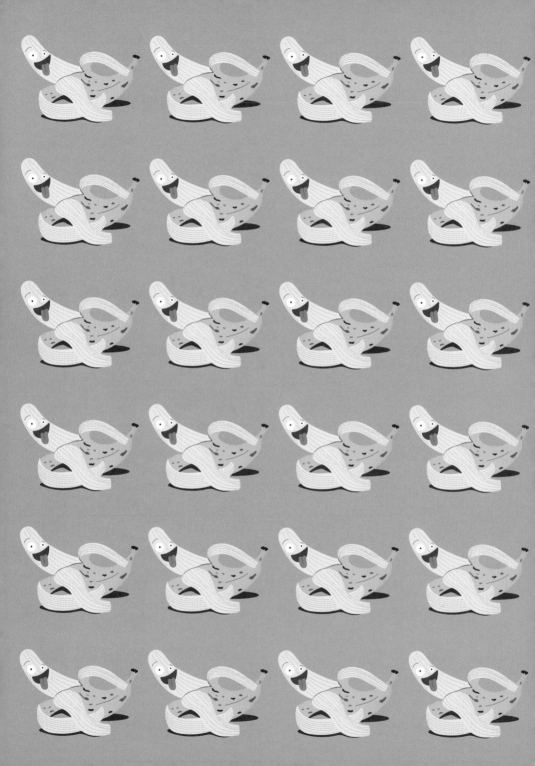

THE ILLUSTRATED Compendium =OF= Essential MODERN SLANG

LEGIT · YOLO · extra · SHOOK · LIT

Including Cray, Lit, Basic, and More

by Tyler Vendetti

Illustrated by Rebecca Pry

For Cody Vendetti.
(Third time's the charm, right?)

13-digit ISBN: 978-1-95151-102-9
10-digit ISBN: 1-95151-102-6

This book may be ordered by mail from the publisher. Please include $5.99 for postage and handling. Please support your local bookseller first!

Books published by Whalen Book Works are available at special discounts when purchased in bulk. For more information, please email us at info@whalenbookworks.com.

Whalen Book Works
68 North Street
Kennebunkport, ME 04046

www.whalenbookworks.com

Cover and interior design by Melissa Gerber
Typography: Times New Roman, Adobe Caslon, ITC Caslon 224, Minya Nouvelle Italic, Times LT STD, and Times.

Printed in China
1 2 3 4 5 6 7 8 9 0

First Edition

INTRODUCTION

There comes a point in everyone's life when they realize they're officially old. For some, it's the day their doctor explains, with a disappointed sigh, that "you're not in your twenties anymore." For others, it's the cacophony of cracking bones that rings out after a morning stretch. For me, it was the feeling of utter bewilderment that engulfed my body when my brother, a mere five years younger than me, used a slang word that I, a self-professed word nerd, did not recognize. In that moment, a wave of anxious thoughts flooded my mind. Had I not spent enough time on the internet, swapping memes with youths in an attempt to stay relevant? Is this what my mother felt like when I tried to teach her how to use Snapchat? Was my sibling, a notorious trickster, inventing a term so absurd that my paranoid brain would assume it was real?

As these ideas began swirling around my subconscious, I started taking a closer look at slang and its role in our lives, our culture, and our vocabularies. And boy, did I underestimate just how significant it is.

For one, slang is history's best bookkeeper. You can pluck a slang word from any period of our country's short life and know exactly what was going on during that time. For example, if the term in question is a synonym for booze, then it probably came out during the Prohibition era of the 1920s. If it relates to mental impairment of any kind, you can look to the 1960s and the counterculture movement's love for hallucinogenic substances. If it's a shorthand you might find on your teenager's phone, it likely popped up during the dot-com boom like an AIM away message.

But while slang words may be markers of history, they are also victims of history in that they, too, are affected by time and how it shapes our surroundings. A term that starts out as a derogatory slur may eventually be seized and redefined by the very group it was meant to attack. An innocuous quip may fizzle and then fall dormant for years before resurfacing with a new connotation or, in some cases, an entirely new meaning. An expression that your mother once loved may, in the span of a decade, develop a new context and get her yelled at on the internet, leading her to swear off Facebook and angry-mumble about PC culture.

Though most of these changes can be blamed on teenagers who choose to kill and resurrect jargon as they so please, others are born from larger, cultural trends: viral videos, political events, social media sites, etc. Slang—like fashion or technology or your crush on Derek from math class—changes over time, mutating according to the society it lives in and the people that claim it as their own.

In a way, though, it is this susceptibility to time and the memories it holds that makes slang so universal. No matter how old you are or what generation you belong to, you have, at some point in your life, used slang. This thing that differentiates you from your parents' generation and your grandparents' generation also, at the same time, unites you; it is a reminder that, despite our many differences, one thing that we have in common—that we will always have in common—is language and the ways in which we use that language to memorialize our experiences.

So the next time your brother or sister or five-year-old wiseacre nephew utters a word you've never heard of and you feel the bones in your body creak under the weight of your own aging organs, remember that one day they too will find themselves stumped by the jargon of some Gen Q child and wondering when, exactly, they became one of the dreaded Olds.

How to Use This Book

When we conceived of the idea for this book, there were a few burning questions that we sought to answer. Namely, what sort of words fall under the scope of "essential," especially in a world where our vocabularies change every five seconds? Is it the ones that made a splash when they debuted, lodging themselves into the brains of your parents and grandparents before fading from the country's collective consciousness? Or the ones that enjoyed a soft opening before slipping under the radar, quietly hopping from generation to generation until one day everyone looks around and realizes that the word is, somehow, still here, like the last guy at the dinner party who just won't take the hint and leave.

The answer, we decided, is a little bit of both. While there are some terms like *canary* or *egghead* that are no longer around, their popularity back in the day reflects their historical significance. Which is to say, they were popular for a reason and if we exclude them, we'd also be excluding pieces of our own history. This also explains why words like *swerve* and *banger* have a place in this compendium: they may be long forgotten twenty years from now, but at this moment, they are all the rage, and to ignore that fact would be to ignore the conditions and culture that led to their success in the first place. (And I don't know about you, but we at Whalen Book Works are not in the business of rewriting or burying history.) On the flip side, while words like *blabbermouth* or *malarkey* may not have seen the same success as other lingo initially, their lasting influence on our language have earned them recognition and, in turn, a spot in this fine book.

That said, at the end of the day, *The Illustrated Compendium of Essential Modern Slang* contains only a fraction of our history's best jargon. Why? Because, as I'm sure you know, the world is very old, and capturing every popular word since cavemen walked the earth would require a lot more pages than I've been given permission to write. As a result, I've aimed to limit this book to slang words from the year 1900 and beyond. Can they originate earlier than 1900? Of course. I'm not ageist. But their windows of popularity should fall roughly within the 20th century window to avoid constructing a collection of words from an era whose members are all certainly dead now.

While this book *can* be used as a bible for those new to American culture seeking insight on the nonsense the youth are spewing, I'd suggest using it more like a guidebook that you can consult whenever a teenager makes a confusing remark or a senior citizen shouts some gobbledygook that you suspect is baloney. By this I mean: This book doesn't have all the answers, but it should have enough to help you survive a day in a Midwestern high school, an urban factory, or a coastal nursing home—and really, isn't that all you need?

Pronunciation Guide

At the start of every word in this book, you will find a pronunciation guide filled with symbols that you're *sure* you saw in an Egyptian hieroglyphic once. These wannabe Wingdings are explained in detail below, for your convenience.

Vowels

i = I can't wait for this Chicken Pox Convention **meet** and greet.

i = My two front teeth appear to be lodged in a chunk of saltwater **taffy**.

ɪ = If I hear another teenager say the word **lit**, I swear . . .

ɛ = The **Hess** Truck jingle is stuck in my head again.

ɛ = My name's **Hairy**, but spelled H-A-I-R-Y.

æ = Can someone tell Jason to stop answering every question with a **rap** lyric?

ɑ = I'll be watching you like a **rock**: silently.

ɑ = No, Paris, liquid nitrogen is not **hot**.

ɔ, ɑ = Jack and the **Beanstalk**? More like Jack and the BORING stalk!

ə = I don't want to brag but, I am the regional **cup-stacking** champion.

ʊ = You've got some **soot** on your face. Or is it . . . yeah, it's just a freckle.

u = We were **rooting** for you! We were all rooting for you!

ə = My Dad likes **Metallica**. I don't know what that is, but it sounds cool so I support it, whatever that is.

ɔr = Every school has a **horse** girl. If you can't name one, it's probably you.

ər = Make sure I have a cool **hearse** when I die, OK?

ɪ(ə)r = Don't give me that **deer** in headlights look, Bob.

ɛ(ə)r = I would get out of your **hair**, but I'm stuck. Get the scissors.

ʊ(ə)r = I had my first kiss while listening to The **Cure** and I don't think I've recovered.

eɪ = Does cuddling count as second **base**?

aɪ = Come closer. Does this look like **lice** to you?

aʊ = You've got a **mouth** on you. And a nose, two eyes, some light freckles . . .

oʊ = Where is the **moat** I asked for? And the drawbridge??

ɔɪ = That little **voice** inside your head? It's me. I hacked your hearing aid.

æ̃ = This year, for my mid-life crisis, I'm going to get **bangs**.

ɑ̃ = I'm quite **fond** of you and your little talking dog too.

Consonants

b = **B**ad news. I've gone vegan.

d = Gosh **d**arnit, if that's not the cutest hedgehog I've ever seen.

dʒ = **J**ars are like cups for cool people.

ð = **Th**is whole revolution thing is harder than I thought.

f = **F**irst of all, I never said I was good at cutting hair. Second of all, I'm sorry.

g = **G**osh, I just can't remember your name.

h = Was it **H**arry?

j = Or **Y**orich?

k = **K**evin maybe?

l = **L**isten, I'm bad with names. Can't you just tell me?

m = Oh! It's **M**ark. With a *k*. I got it.

n = This is **n**ot your average Trader Joe's.

ŋ = That's some nice bli**ng** you've got there. Where'd you get it? Jared's?

p = **P**itter-patter, goes the rain.

r = This is more of a mouse race than a **r**at race, if you ask me.

s = No **s**hoes, no shirt, no problem: welcome to the nudist colony.

ʃ = Skunk scent got you down? Just **sh**ake it off.

t = **T**alk to the hand because the face is too tired to listen, frankly.

tʃ = **Ch**ocolate ice cream is lame. What about boisenberry ice cream?

θ = **Th**e right answer is usually a woman's.

v = **V**iolence is not the answer either. Margaritas are the answer.

w = You **w**in some, you lose some, you sleep through some.

z = **Z**ip-a-dee-doo-dah, zip-a-dee-day. My oh my, it's been a very long day.

ʒ = I envi**s**ion a future where people *and* vending machines are free.

x = **Lo**ch is just lock with a little bit of phlegm thrown in.

Oh, and if you see a ' symbol, don't be alarmed: it just how we indicate where the stress falls so you don't go around saying PO-tay-toes instead of po-TAY-toes.

ace (verb | /eɪs/):

To excel at a certain subject or activity, or a name you might give to your firstborn son in the hope that he'll *ace* everything in his life and make his ol' dad proud.

Origin: Although the verb *ace* was originally used among tennis elites to describe an unreturnable serve, the idiom *ace* came directly from the United States grading system, which measures a student's success in class or on exams with letters (typically, A through F) that correspond to point values. If, for example, a student receives a 95 out of 100 on a test, they will get an A (meaning they have *aced* the test). If they get an 84 out of 100, they will get a B. If they get a 3 out of 100, they probably slept through the test by accident and got 3 pity points from their teacher who didn't have the heart to give them a flat out zero.

"I may be a first-grader but I have already aced my ABCs."

adult (verb | /əˈdəlt/):

Crippled by student debt and a crumbling job market, young people these days are considered lucky if they are able to support themselves by the time they're in their thirties, which explains why the word *adulting* (completing a grown-up task) has recently exploded in popularity; so rarely do millennials get the opportunity to feel like adults that they had to invent a whole new word to help them describe such moments.

Origin: *Adulting* or *to adult* was born in 2008, when college graduates across the United States were heading out in search of jobs and finding . . . well, nothing. The Great Recession of 2008 left many twentysomethings with lots of bills and little opportunity, forcing many to move back in with parents who didn't understand why their kids, shackled with 800-dollar-a-month loans, were not "starting families" or "buying houses" or "spending money" or whatever.

> **❝**I adulted so hard this week. I paid off one of my college loans. One down, fifteen to go!**❞**

aesthetic (noun | /ɛsˈθɛdɪk/):

The kind of personal brand that someone might carefully curate on their Instagram page in order to convey a particular vibe like "girl who pets cats at parties" or "Hollywood eccentric."

Origin: *Aesthetic* goes back to the eighteenth century, when German philosopher Alexander Baumgarten began to outline a system of principles for the appreciation of art and beauty. Hundreds of years later, in the 2010s, vaporwave musicians took this concept and gave it a face-lift by using it to describe the very specific "look" of their electro-pop subgenre. The collective internet took this concept mainstream, as Tumblrs and blogs customized with a certain aesthetic began popping up online.

66 Everything on Britney's Instagram page has a pink tinge to it. Either she's trying to build an aesthetic, or her camera's broken. **99**

amped (adjective | /æmptʹ/):

Excited or energetic, like the sound your guitar makes every time you plug it into a literal amp.

Origin: Speaking of guitar amps, that's where this word originates: from rock stars or wannabe rock stars plugging in their instruments during concerts and watching the crowd come alive with the music. (There are other theories that suggest the word came from amphetamines, but you can consult the internet for those.)

66 Blink 182 is playing at my college this weekend and I'm amped. I mean, it's not really Blink 182, it's a cover band, but still. **99**

ankle-biter (noun | /ˈæŋk(ə)l ˌbaɪdər/):

If you think poodles are bad, just wait until an ankle-biter gets in your home. Known for their high-pitched screams and putrid scents, these creatures have infiltrated houses across the United States. They're also frequently referred to as *toddlers* and avoiding them is highly encouraged.

Origin: First appearing in an 1850 publication of *Harper's Magazine*, *ankle-biter* resurfaced in the 1950s, defining a generation of post-WWII dads who were discovering just how difficult babies really were.

> **"**Has anyone fed the ankle-biter today? No, not the dog, the other one. The thing that looks like us.**"**

antsville (noun | /æntsvɪl/):

A crowded place, like every store you walk into when you're in a hurry, somehow.

Origin: A product of the linguistic trend that saw *-ville* tacked onto the end of everything, *antsville* arose in the 1950s and was likely the result of an era defined by socialization. Which is to say, the economic boom following WWII allowed teenagers to enter the world of leisure: school dances, drive-ins, and diners all became hot spots for fresh-faced baby boomers and for a while, the world seemed packed with people, milling around with their friends like little ants.

> **"**This place is antsville, I can't even hear my own thoughts. Let's hit Johnny Rockets and call it a day, boys.**"**

applesauce (noun | /ˈæp(ə)lsɑs/):

Nonsense! Crazy talk! Why are we yelling?

Origin: This expression, often used in anger by the elderly, first appeared around the 1920s, though no one can seem to decide on when. Some sources claim the word's first mention was in 1919 in a piece by cartoonist T. A. Dorgen ("They spill a lot of applesauce about big money"). Others point to *Collier's Magazine*, where the word appeared in both a 1920 and 1921 print issue.

awesomesauce

(adjective | /ˈɔsəm ˌsɔs/):

Extremely good or excellent; the opposite of what one thinks when they hear this word in conversation.

Origin: It's the year 2000 and the cartoon *Homestar Runner* has hit the internet. Strong Bad, the red-faced star, was the first to use this atrocious word. (See, parents? You were right. Cartoons *are* ruining this generation!)

baddie (noun | /ˈbædi/):

In the 1930s, baddie meant "criminal." In the 1940s, it meant "movie villain." Now, it means someone who failed at self-restraint and had three cookies in a row, causing them to shamefully announce to their friends "I'm *so* bad!"

Origin: Per the *Oxford English Dictionary*, *baddie* first showed up in a 1934 issue of the *Daily News Standard Post*, appearing in a sentence that sounds like the start of a dystopian novel for three-year-olds: "Both the goodies and the baddies have influence now."

❝ They've finally announced the name of the next Spiderman reboot! *Spiderman: Revenge of the Baddies.* ❞

bae (noun | /beɪ/):

A significant other, the kind that you put Before Anyone Else and cuddle with on rainy days.

Origin: We can blame memes for this. In 2013, a meme featuring people taking pictures of themselves as if they were taken by their significant others gained traction online. The caption for those pictures? "Bae caught me slippin'." You had to be there.

❝ Hey, bae. You still coming over tonight? I've got the Scrabble board and wine all set up. ❞

baggage (noun | /ˈbægɪdʒ/):

Everyone has baggage: qualities or experiences that are perceived to bring down the carrier and those that the carrier interacts with. For some, it's family baggage (messy divorce, testy parents, seven bratty children). For others, it's emotional baggage (being guarded, selfish, neglectful). For many, it's literal baggage (broken suitcases and overloaded carry-ons).

Origin: Though this interpretation of the word became popular in the 1950s, it has actually been around for much longer than that—since the 1600s, to be exact. Though the "baggage" of the 1600s was likely very different from the baggage we have today (soul-crushing colonialism versus soul-crushing student debt), at the end of the day, it all hurts just the same.

bail (verb | /beɪl/):

To leave somewhere quickly, like when you're in prison and your mom comes to make your bail so you rush out as fast as possible before any of your macho prison friends can see; to cancel plans unexpectedly and without notice, probably because you just went to jail and are waiting for your mom to bail you out.

Origin: Nearly every definition of bail somehow relates to the same basic principle: getting one thing out of another thing. Bailing out a sinking ship means you're scooping water out of the boat and back into the ocean. Bailing someone out of jail means you're removing them from a cell. Bailing on your friend means you are going to get a very angry text in about an hour when the networking event you promised to attend with them finally ends. The term most likely came from the old phrase *bail out,* which refers to soldiers who jump out of (and therefore abandon) aircrafts.

baller (noun | /ˈbɔlər/):

Someone who spends money freely and ostentatiously, even if they probably shouldn't be spending money freely and ostentatiously.

Origin: *Baller* has been used since the seventeenth century to refer to people who formally play ball, but its use as a slang word originated in the early twentieth century when athletes started referring to themselves by their sport (baseballers, basketballers, footballers). In the 1980s, with the rise of celebrity basketball stars and their unlimited wallets, *ballers* quickly became associated with rich sports players and their unchecked spending.

❝ You have three basketball courts on your property? Two for pickup games and one for raining money on? That's baller. ❞

baloney (noun | /bəˈloʊni/):

Nonsense. See: *applesauce* (page 13) or anything your Grandpa Joe says.

Origin: First used by former New York governor Alfred E. Smith in the 1930s to criticize the presidential policies of Franklin D. Roosevelt, Smith was once quoted saying, "No matter how thin you slice it, it's still baloney." From there, the phrase took off.

❝ *Bologna* is spelled with a *g*? That's baloney. ❞

bananas (adjective | /bəˈnænəs/):

Crazy, like people who enjoy the taste of bananas.

Origin: Unclear. Though some studies say this word gained popularity in the 1970s, there are many earlier instances of it, some relating the term to the slang phrase *to go ape* (apes eat bananas and apes can act crazy; therefore, *bananas* equals crazy) and others relating the term to the 1924 phrase *banana oil*.

66 This banana is *bananas*, man. Look at it! It's so yellow and curvy! 99

banger (noun | /ˈbæŋər/):

A catchy song that makes you want to dance like no one's watching.

Origin: Interestingly, this word appeared in the 1970s to describe head-banging concertgoers who, in response to the music, would bang their heads up and down. You know, to really feel the music. The rise and fall of certain genres (techno, hip-hop, whatever Gangnam Style was) has brought this word in and out of relevance.

66 That yodeling kid has a new song out. He coughs up some phlegm, like, a minute in. It's a real banger. 99

bash (noun | /bæʃ/):

A big ol' party.

Origin: There are theories that the word *bash* comes from Australia, New Zealand, or the United Kingdom, but one of the earliest known uses of *bash* actually comes from the US. Back in the 1900s, *to go on a bash* was used to describe a "drunken spree," and it's believed that the "celebration" sense of the word stemmed from here. A personal theory: *bash* could also come from the knee-jerk desire to bash one's head in after a hangover-inducing bash the night before.

❝Don't bash my birthday bash, Baxter.❞

basic (adjective | /ˈbeɪsɪk/):

Enjoying mainstream food, clothes, or trends so much that you shed any sense of uniqueness and become a cookie-cutter human being. Basic people can be found standing in line at Starbucks, tuning the radio to the local "Top 40" station, or standing by the coffee machine chatting about whatever summer blockbuster just came out.

Origin: *Basic* in the "that girl is so basic" sense first appeared in 1985, exploding in popularity following the release of the 1984 song "Meeting in the Ladies Room" by Klymaxx, in which a woman is criticized for hitting on the singer's boyfriend. The word saw a resurgence in the 2000s with the rise of the pumpkin spice latte and Longchamp bags.

❝Basic women rarely make history.❞

beat (verb / adjective | /bit/):

As a verb: to apply makeup heavily, to defeat, or to physically attack. As an adjective: worn-out or tired, like someone literally beat the energy out of you.

Origin: Not entirely sure, but most guess that it's related to the physical action of being beaten which, frankly, is exhausting.

> 66 I can't go to the rubber ducky convention today, man. I'm just too beat from work. 99

beef (noun | /bif/):

A complaint or vendetta; a type of meat so delicious that it stops aspiring vegans in their tracks.

Origin: *Beef* started as a verb meaning "to grumble or gripe" back in 1888. A decade or so later, it was noun-ified to refer to a general complaint. This lingo likely originated with the United States Army, whose soldiers were known for criticizing the poor quality of their beef rations, though some believe it may instead come from the old cockney rhyme "hot beef!," which was used to mock marketplace sellers who would attempt to call out "stop, thief!" when a robber swiped their produce in the streets.

> 66 What's your beef with beef, Nancy? Bessie here tastes delicious to me. 99

bestie (noun | /ˈbɛsti/):

A best friend; someone who you can share deeply intimate moments with one second and highly descriptive accounts of your last bowel movement with the next.

Origin: The first recorded account of the word occurred in 1991 in a British newspaper, but it had been circulating among young people for years prior, often interchangeably with *BFF*, *biffle*, and "brother from another mother."

> **❝**Are you my bestie or just a friendie? Or, like, an acquaintancie? I need to know how to list you on my MySpace Top 5.**❞**

bible (noun | /ˈbʌɪb(ə)l/):

The court system could expedite their process by swapping the whole "I do solemnly and sincerely and truly declare and affirm that the evidence I shall give shall be the truth, the whole truth, and nothing but the truth" vow with one simple word: *bible*. The term is a product of the 2010s and is used to signify that a piece of information is, hand to God, true.

Origin: The world can thank *Keeping Up with the Kardashians* for this lingo. Or, rather, we can thank whatever two brothers Kourtney and Kim dated in high school: the sisters claim their old flames used to use the word at family gatherings, and it stuck with them ever since.

> **❝**Do you think this dress makes me look fat? Say bible!**❞**

B

bigwig (noun | /ˈbɪɡˌwɪɡ/):

A noteworthy person, the kind that others whisper conspiratorially about when they walk into a room at parties.

Origin: During the eighteenth century, wig-wearing had become more than just a fashion trend; it was a status symbol. The bigger the wig, the more expensive it was, and the richer the person wearing it likely was, inspiring the word *bigwig* to represent these Very Important People.

> ❝ Napoleon, you think just because you led several successful campaigns during the French Revolutionary War that you're a bigwig, huh? Get real. ❞

binge (verb | /bɪndʒ/):

To binge, in the modern sense, means to view multiple episodes of television or media back to back, in one sitting, in pajamas, surrounded by snacks, without moving or blinking or using the bathroom unless it's absolutely, positively necessary.

Origin: *Binge* is a curious word that dates back to the 1800s, where it was used to describe soaking wood in water and, later, soaking people in alcohol (a.k.a. getting very, very inebriated). From there, the term snowballed into binge-drinking, binge-reading, binge-watching, and eventually simply bingeing.

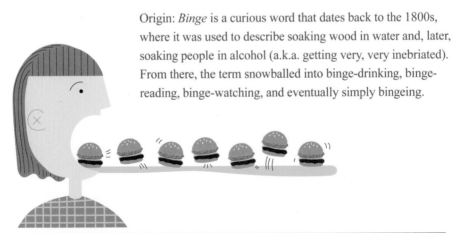

bippy (noun | /ˈbɪpi/):
The buttocks, respectively.

Origin: Before the days of *SNL*, there was a sketch comedy show called *Rowan & Martin's Laugh-In* on NBC that often featured nonsense words that writers thought would garner a laugh. One such word was *bippy,* which aired one night as part of the quip "You bet your sweet bippy!," When later asked about the show's use of confusing "fake words," executive producer George Schlatter responded: "What upsets most of the critics are the jokes they don't understand, and that's more of an educational problem than a taste problem."

❝Bippity, boppity, boo! That's one fine bippy!❞

bird (verb | /bərd/):

What's slower than driving, faster than walking, and guaranteed to make you the most hated member of your community? An electric scooter! Find one on your nearby street corner, thrown carelessly aside, like your dreams.

Origin: Though the first electric scooter was technically invented in 1915 (it was called the Autoped and looked like something you might find at a yard sale), e-scooters didn't go mainstream until 2012, when Scoot Networks launched the first short-range scooter rental system. The business really boomed, though, when Birds hit the scene in 2017, branding themselves as the first dockless scooters in the area. And that, kids, is how birding was born.

> 66 Let's see. The concert venue is thirty minutes away. Is there a way we can get there that's both cheap *and* makes us look cool? Oh wait. We could bird! 99

blabbermouth (noun | /ˈblæbərˌmaʊθ/):

Someone who talks far too much and loud enough for the gossipmonger three buildings down to hear. Hope you don't mind the world knowing about that fungus you contracted last week.

Origin: A combination of *blabber* and *mouth* that was invented in the 1930s, likely by a lost lush who wouldn't stop yelling, "Now where exactly did you say that Prohibition bar was?"

66 The heist was going swimmingly, until Darryl started chatting with one of the security guards about all the money he was going to make. That's the last time I hire a blabbermouth . . . 99

blast (noun | /blæst/):

A good time, usually in a party sense, as in "Amelia's wedding to her fourth husband was a real blast."

Origin: An Americanism from the 1950s, suggesting that, perhaps, post-WWII soldiers were trying to put a positive spin on "blasts" and "explosions."

❝No, I'm not crying. I'm having a blast! These are happy tears!❞

blessed (adjective | /blɛst/):

Lucky or grateful. This slang word is only valid if preceded by a hashtag and posted ironically on social media.

Origin: The exact origin is difficult to pinpoint, but one of the earliest uses of *blessed* as a slang word was 2011, when a music vlogger wrote that the rapper Lil B was "#rare, very #based, and [that] we are all #blessed for his presence." From then on, people began to use #blessed as a semi-sarcastic way of expressing gratitude for everything, from big wins ("I'm feeling #blessed for this Grammy award") to the small ones ("I arrived two minutes after happy hour ended but the waiter gave me the discounted wine flight anyway, so I'm feeling really #blessed this evening").

❝I stopped hanging out with Edgar. Ever since he got a Twitter, he would not stop saying 'hashtag blessed' after every tiny accomplishment. Even in real life, out loud.❞

bling (noun | /blɪŋ/):

Flashy jewelry, like diamond chains, ruby rings, or silver necklaces donning annoying words like "swag" in big, obnoxiously shiny letters.

Origin: Everyone knew the name Cash Money Millionaires in the 1990s. They were a rap group out of New Orleans composed of Big Tymer$ (Birdman and Mannie Fresh) and the Hot Boy$ (B.G., Juvenile, Lil Wayne, and Turk). In 1999, one of the members, B.G., released a song called "Bling Bling" that introduced the concept *bling*.

❝Do you think I'm wearing enough bling? Should I add another peacock brooch?❞

blue (adjective | /blu/):

When someone says, "I feel blue," they're not talking about the color. They're talking about the emotion of feeling "blue," also known by common folk as "sad."

Origin: *Blue* in the depressed sense was first recorded in 1741 and was possibly in reference to *blue devil*, an archaic term for a baleful demon. It may have also come from Chaucer, who was one of the first to use this term in his 1385 piece *Complaint of Mars*. Somehow, the meaning stuck, all the way up until 1998, when Eiffel 65 released its hit song "I'm Blue" and cemented its popularity in our vocabularies for years to come.

❝ I'm blue. No, not literally. Emotionally. **❞**

bod (noun | /bad/):

A playful term for "body," shortened from four letters to three thanks to our
dwindling attention spans.

Origin: *Bod* has drifted in and out of our vocabulary for decades and has signified
everything from "a surfer dude" to "corpse" to "Beginning of Day." In its most
recent iteration, *bod* refers to someone's physique, which can range from "hot
bod" to "sad bod" to everyone's favorite: "dad bod."

> **❝❝**Check out that guy's *bod*. *Someone's* been hitting the StairMaster.**❞❞**

bogart (verb | /ˈboʊˌgart/):

To hog something greedily or selfishly; what
your partner does with the bed blankets on a
cold winter night, leaving you to shiver like a
worm without its dirt.

Origin: Humphrey Bogart was one of the
greatest actors of our time and was arguably
the face of the 1940s film noir movement,
headlining classic movies like *The Maltese
Falcon* and *The Big Sleep*. Thanks to this, he
often played characters that were considered
stereotypically tough, like gangsters and
private detectives. Adding to this gritty image
was Bogart's use of cigarettes; he'd always have one dangling from his mouth as he
spoke, a move that quickly became his trademark and inspired the 1960s notion of
keeping a joint in the mouth instead of passing it on. This selfish move eventually
became synonymous with the man who created it, thus leading to the verb *to bogart*.

bogus (noun | /ˈboʊɡəs/):

Something that is made up or fake, like the story you keep telling everyone about that scar on your left cheek. A hippopotamus attack isn't exactly convincing.

Origin: Interestingly, *bogus* originally referred to a machine used to counterfeit coins in the 1800s by impressing patterns into metal. These devices, used to generate fake money, became associated with fake things in general, and the word is now used to refer to fake people, fake stories, fake music festivals, you name it.

❝This pyramid scheme is bogus.❞

bomb (verb | /bɑm/):

To fail at something badly, like, say, choosing a box of chocolates instead of a wedding ring for your girlfriend of five years on Valentine's Day.

Origin: *Bomb* as a noun has been around since, well, since the bomb was invented in the 1580s. The verb, though, didn't show up until the 1960s and possibly appeared in reference to machines that were "bombing out," a.k.a. glitching.

❝I bombed that calculus test this morning. Like, my grade is going to go up in literal flames.❞

boogie (verb | /ˈbʊgi/):

To dance and sing and drink and keep drinking and fall down the stairs and crawl into bed and wake up with a headache and promise to never dance/sing/drink/etc. ever again. Can also mean "to leave quickly," which is exactly what you might do in the aforementioned scenario.

Origin: In 1929, Will Ezell released a song called "Pitchin' Boogie" in which he describes a girl who "can boogie too mean." Later, in the 1970s, the proliferation of songs with names like "Boogie Wonderland," "Boogie Nights," and "Boogie Shoes" led to this word's comeback and its association with America's most unfortunate contribution to the music scene: disco.

❝ What do you want to do tonight, sweetie? Get ice cream? Watch a movie? Boogie? ❞

book (verb | /bʊk/):

To leave in a hurry, either because you're bored, tired, or suddenly concerned about seeing someone you know from high school.

Origin: Though some have suggested this word came about due to its similarity to *boogie*, it's more likely that it originated in the United States Army, where soldiers were required to sign a logbook upon entering or leaving a company area.

❝ This library is lame. Let's book it outta here. ❞

boonies (noun | /ˈbuniz/):

The middle of nowhere; a term for a nothing-to-do town.

Origin: Another United States Army term that sprang up during the Vietnam era to describe any forested place outside of Saigon. Eventually, "any forested place outside of Saigon" became "any forested place outside," then "anywhere rural," and finally "anywhere boring."

❝ There's only one movie theater in this town, and it only offers back-to-back showings of *Transformers: The Last Knight*. God, I hate the boonies. ❞

bougie (adjective | /ˈbu(d)ʒi/):

A word to describe your friend who knows resort fees better than she knows her own name and who refuses to buy any food that's not preceded by "organic." In the dictionary, you'd find it under the definition for *pretentious* or *ritzy*.

Origin: Stemming from the French word *bourgeoisie* ("middle class status"), *bougie* eventually became synonymous with materialism and people who give their dogs royal names like Sir Edward or Baron.

> **❝** I heard she paid one hundred thousand dollars on a Polaroid of a cherry stapled to a wall. She's too bougie for me. **❞**

bounce (verb | /baʊns/):

To leave quickly and suddenly, before anyone can hear you use the word *bounce*.

Origin: Poets, take note: *bounce* is a word of many uses (i.e., to bounce ideas around, to receive a bounceback, to get kicked out of New York's hottest club by a big scary bouncer). The "I gotta bounce" usage, though, didn't hit the streets until the 1980s and was likely derived from an older use of the word bounce: to expel or to come and go unceremoniously like a tossed ball.

> **❝** This party's whack, homie. Let's bounce like a slinky on a staircase. **❞**

brewski (noun | /ˈbruski/):

A bro-y term for beer that's likely plastered across the wall of frat houses across the country.

Origin: A combination of *brew* (colloquialism for "brewed beer") and *-ski* (a Slavic suffix that can be found on the last name of your most Polish friend) that was born in the 1970s along with your parents.

    ❝I'm gonna grab a brewski with the gang before I boogie over to my crib and crash.❞

broke (adjective | /broʊk/):

To be woefully out of money and unable to buy that hip technological device that you've had pinned to your vision board for months.

Origin: It seems that *broke* in the penniless sense evolved from *broken* or *break* which, in the seventeenth century, meant "to financially ruin," as in "These ticket prices for the upcoming Harry Styles concert are breaking me."

    ❝It's like, I would love to buy some Synergy Kombucha, but I already bought the Enlightened Kombucha yesterday, so I'm totally broke.❞

bromance (noun | /ˈbroʊˌmæns/):

When a man falls platonically in love with another man, what results is a bromance—a meaningful friendship involving late night *Call of Duty* tournaments, shared spousal complaints, and a long list of stories from semi-dangerous shenanigans that are never disclosed beyond the larger bro wolf pack.

Origin: *Bromance* or *bro-romance* was first coined in the 1990s by Dave Carnie to describe the relationship formed between skaters. The term took on a life of its own during the 2000s, though, and quickly became adopted by Hollywood as its own subgenre, spawning male-skewing buddy comedies and adventure films like *The Hangover* and *Wedding Crashers*.

❝ The results are in! The top three bromances in history are 'Frodo and Sam,' 'Matt Damon and Ben Affleck,' and 'your dad and the bartender from Chili's'! ❞

brony (noun | /'broʊni/):

An adult male who enjoys watching *My Little Pony*, the animated television series inspired by the popular Hasbro toys that features anthropomorphic horses with names like Twilight Sparkle, Applejack, and Rainbow Dash prancing through Ponyville in search of love, laughter, and friendship. Did I mention that these were adult males? I did, right?

Origin: Though the toys have been around since the 1980s, the *My Little Pony* series did not debut until 2010, at which point, users of the popular Reddit-like site 4chan launched a series of message boards to discuss the adventures of these bubble-gum creatures. The popularity of such fan groups snowballed, eventually leading to the creation of BronyCon (a brony convention) and numerous brony documentaries. Why are men the leaders of this MLP craze? Unclear. Many self-identifying bronies insist that the show exists on multiple planes, with jokes catering to kids but also to adults, while others point to the built-in nostalgia of a show adapted from a classic '80s toy, but neither argument explains how gender plays into their pony obsession.

> ❝Dude, did you read that fan fiction on the brony board about Rainbow Dash and Applejack starting an auto body shop in Detroit? It was one of the best pieces I read this year.❞

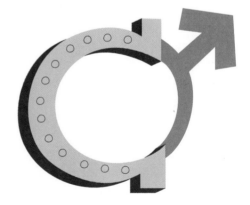

brouhaha (noun | /ˈbruˌhaˌha/):

A small commotion, like the kind happening at the dinner table right now over a black and blue (or is it white and gold?) dress.

Origin: Unclear. Though some linguists think the word is onomatopoeic in origin (a.k.a. a group of bickering guys produced a cacophony of noise that sounded like "brouhaha"), others claim it comes from the Hebrew phrase *bārŪkh habbā'* ("blessed be he who enters"), which inexperienced worshippers mispronounced as "brouhaha," causing experienced worshippers to mock them and cause one of those little commotions we were talking about.

❝ There was a big brouhaha over which coffee shop we should go to after I mentioned that Starbucks had better cold brew than Dunkin' Donuts. Guess that's what I get for being friends with Bostonians. ❞

bug (verb | /bəg/):

To irritate; to flee in a panic; to behave in an irrational way; to install a concealed microphone in someone else's space in order to eavesdrop on their conversations, only to realize they spend most of their day cursing inanimate objects for being in the way and chatting with friends on the phone about what IKEA discounts they got in the mail that week.

Origin: This word has so many meanings in the English language that it would be hard to list all of their origins here, but a good place to start would be the phrase *bug out*, which originated among American soldiers during the Korean War. When troops found themselves in a compromising position, they were sometimes told to "bug out" (a.k.a. scatter like bugs) in order to escape the danger quickly and find new footing. Somewhere along the way, this definition changed, morphing into a term for panicked thinking instead of just panicked movement. The 1995 movie *Clueless* adopted this idea, introducing the catchphrase "totally buggin'" that fans of the cult film have definitely abused.

❝Now, don't bug out, but there's a giant spider nestling into your earlobe.❞

bummer (noun | /ˈbəmər/):

A disappointment, like your decision to major in the arts, according to your parents.

Origin: From the English adjective *bum* meaning "of poor quality." Its noun counterpart arrived in the 1960s, and for some reason, never left.

❝Pants without snack pockets are such a bummer.❞

burned (adjective | /bəːnd/):

To be mocked so badly that one's body physically hurts, like it's been singed by a hot flame.

Origin: Though *burn* in the insult sense has been around for decades (and likely formed from the literal meaning of burn as "a painful injury caused by something hot"), its place in the slang world solidified with the debut of *That '70s Show* in 1998 and Kelso's frequent and obnoxious deployment of the word in response to stinging jabs.

❝I just got burned by my younger sister. Verbally and literally she mocked my pants before setting them on fire.❞

bust (verb | /bəst/):

To catch someone in the act, like when police bust a thief robbing a bank or when you bust your sister stealing your favorite tank top from your closet again.

Origin: A variant of the word *burst* meaning "break open or expose."

cakewalk (noun | /ˈkeɪk ˌwɔk/):

An easy, often one-sided task and also a word we should probably retire. See below.

Origin: The word *cakewalk* has a long and troubling history. First appearing in the nineteenth century, a cakewalk was originally a dance conducted by African American slaves to mock the formal dancing of white plantation owners. Entertained by these rituals, slave owners started holding competitions called "cakewalks" and promised slices of cake to the slave with the fanciest footwork.

> **❝** That cookie-decorating competition was a cakewalk. Was it because I was the only person who showed up? Maybe. But I still won and that's what matters. **❞**

canary <small>(noun | /kəˈnɛri/):</small>

A female singer, the likes of which you might find "chirping" along at the front of the jazzy musical group that your mom hired for your bat mitzvah.

Origin: Everyone knows about the cool cats of the 1930s (the suave male musicians that played saxophone in the basement of every smoky Prohibition bar your grandpa hung out in), but not many people talk about the women who also helped blaze a path for the genre. These female singers were called "canaries" after the incredible tonal range that resembled the effortless warbling of their aviary counterparts.

> **❝ I'm just a cool cat standing in front of a cute canary asking her to love him! ❞**

cancel (verb | /ˈkansəl/):

To reject someone or something because they are no longer trendy or because they did something bad. People who have been canceled include Woody Allen, Lena Dunham, Scarlett Johansson, and that uncle you love that said something racist at Thanksgiving then got mad at you for being mad, resulting in a mutual cancellation.

Origin: The idea of canceling has been around for quite a while (canceling bad TV shows, canceling plans, canceling magazine subscriptions after you realize you haven't looked at a magazine in a decade), but its application toward people is relatively new. Sources suggest this new "cancel culture" was born with the launch of the #MeToo movement, which aimed to expose corrupt figures and hold them accountable for their behavior. Since then, everyone from predatory businessmen to annoying pop stars have been left open to cancellation for their various misdeeds.

catfish (verb | /kætfɪʃ/):

To lie about one's identity online in the hopes of starting a romantic relationship and/or murdering someone (most likely).

Origin: Coined by the husband of Angela Pierce, the subject of the 2010 documentary *Catfish* that tracked one woman's attempt to seduce filmmaker Nev Schulman into a relationship using a slew of fake online personas. Angela, he said, reminded him of ancient fishermen who used to put overactive catfish in the tanks of cod during long journeys in order to keep the cod on their (metaphorical) toes.

❝I accidentally catfished my mom on Facebook the other day. We've had a lot of awkward dinners since then.❞

cheaters (noun | /ˈtʃiːtəs/):

Similar to *peepers*, *cheaters* is a cutesy way of saying "eyeglasses" or "sunglasses," and is used exclusively by adults over the age of fifty.

Origin: Many people seem to believe the term originated in the poker world, where players could cheat by looking at the reflection of someone's glasses to see what cards they were holding. Though this is certainly an entertaining definition, it's more likely that the word refers to glasses' ability to help users "cheat" their bad vision.

❝ Hey, Scooby? Have you seen my cheaters anywhere? ❞

chicken (noun | /ˈtʃɪkən/):

Someone who drops out of an activity due to fear and is subsequently mocked by friends who run around in circles flapping their arms like wings and shouting, "BOCK BOCK BOCK" to really drive home the humiliation.

Origin: Although some attribute the "scaredy-cat" definition of the word to the general tendency for real-life chickens to scamper around nervously, it appears the first mention of the word dates back to the 1600s, in William Kemp's *Nine Days' Wonder*: "It did him good to have ill words of a hoddy doddy! a hebber de hoy! a chicken! a squib." The meaning stuck, and was eventually bolstered by the rise of the devilish game Chicken, which involves driving two cars toward each other at fast speeds until one of them calls it quits and swerves away to avoid dying in a fiery wreck.

chill (adjective / verb | /tʃɪl/):

Shorthand for "laid-back and trustworthy" or "acceptable." As a verb: to relax or, as the kids say, chillax.

Origin: First used by the Sugarhill Gang in their 1979 song "Rapper's Delight," the term has since been reappropriated for the modern age to describe relaxing on the couch, binge-watching a TV show, and not worrying about the inevitably long Monday that awaits.

chrome dome (noun | /kroʊmdoʊm/):

A bald-headed man whose skin is so reflective, it runs the risk of blinding nearby drivers and pedestrians.

Origin: A 1950s slang word used to describe the hairstyle of some soldiers who would shave their heads so close to the scalp, they appeared bald or balding.

❝I don't date chrome domes. I can't stand seeing my own reflection in their forehead every time they lean in for a kiss.**❞**

clapback (noun | /klæpbæk/):

A quippy or stinging retort that usually results in someone shouting "BURRNNNNNNN." (In fact, see: *burn*.)

Origin: Unsurprisingly, this response surfaced in the hip-hop world in 2003 with the release of Ja Rule's appropriately titled diss track "Clap Back," in which he slings shade at Eminem and 50 Cent. The word *clap* itself is a slang word for "to shoot," in reference to the sound of a handgun going off.

❝ Jaden Smith clapbacked to his haters on Twitter by simply posting a selfie from his shiny new yacht. ❞

clock (verb | /klɑk/):

To throw a punch; to notice something or someone, like the private detective in your friend's screenplay who keeps "clocking" suspicious people throughout the story.

Origin: There are some theories, but the main one points to the literal definition of a clock as a timekeeping device. When most people refer to a clock, they are talking about the clock's face—the little circle that we all look at to check the time. This was eventually extended to refer to a human face, so "to clock" someone's face was to notice or look at their face, just as we would notice or look at a clock's face to register the time of day.

❝ Humphrey balanced his cigarette between his lips, scanning the bar for any suspicious persons. That's when he clocked the femme fatale in the corner, who was eyeing him like a fox gearing up for a kill. ❞

clout (noun | /klaʊt/):

Social status that is determined by one's popularity (especially on the internet), like a credit score for coolness. Your brother who has 75,000 followers on Twitter because a joke he made went viral once? He has clout. Your grandmother who has three followers, two of which are her old Twitter accounts that she forgot the password to? No clout. Physical objects can also boost one's clout (which one internet user described as a mix of popularity and notoriety): expensive shoes, VIP tables at a hot club, a phone filled with celebrity contacts that you've interacted with once. All clout boosters.

Origin: In 2008, there was an app called Klout that gave scores to users based on the combined number of Twitter, Instagram, and Facebook followers they had. This score was put on a leaderboard that was said to determine the strength of someone's online influence. Though the app was eventually acquired and forced into a slow, sad death, its legacy has survived in the form of this slang word.

❝ Yeah man, I got clout. I posted one picture of my cat yesterday and Taylor Swift DMed me asking if I'd join her squad. ❞

clutch (noun | /klətʃ/):

Not your mama's handbag, *clutch* in the slang sense refers to a solid performance in a crucial situation, or, more generally, "excellent."

Origin: Clutch is a sports term dating back to the 1920s that describes the critical moment or play that will clinch the win, putting the game in one team's control or "clutch." Most often used in baseball, the word evolved to mean someone or something that is desirable or simply excellent.

copacetic (adjective | /kəʊpəˈsɛtɪk/):

In excellent order. What you can say to your mom next time she asks you how your bedroom looks.

Origin: Truly, no one knows. Its origins have been speculated by at least a dozen journalists, all of which offer very little evidence for their claims. Among the popular theories is that famous dancer Bill Bojangles Robinson invented the term during his run in the 1900s. Others think that two commonly used Yiddish phrases—*hakol b'seder* ("all is in order") and *kol b'tzedek* ("all with justice")—inspired this similar sounding term while some claim it comes from the Chinook word *copasenee* ("everything is satisfactory") instead. Despite all of these theories, the one thing everyone can agree on is that the term is definitely American, as it seems to hardly be recognized outside of North America, which is probably for the best.

> 66 Nothing to see here, coppers. Everything's copacetic. No illegal activity in here. No way. 99

cougar (noun | /ˈkugər/):

An older woman who has a taste for younger men and/or a wild animal who has a taste for flesh. Both will eat you alive, but only one will cuddle and watch human trafficking documentaries with you beforehand.

Origin: Supposedly, *cougar* originated somewhere in Western Canada as a slang word to describe older women who would stalk around bars at night looking for younger men to woo. The term was so popular, it eventually spawned a dating site: CougarDate.com. (And yes, it is still active. Go crazy.)

cowabunga (noun | /ˌkaʊəˈbəŋgə/):

An expression of excitement over good fortune, or the last word your family hears right before you do something really, really stupid.

Origin: Originally stylized as Kowa-Bunga, this exclamation first appeared in a Howdy Doody comic from the 1950s.

> 66 Dude, look at that massive tidal wave. I can't wait to ride that thing. Cowabunga! 99

cram (verb | /kræm/):

To study aggressively and usually last minute.

Origin: It appears that cram in the oh-crap-I-have-an-exam-in-three-hours-and-must-now-memorize-my-entire-textbook sense first appeared in a 1741 self-help book written by Isaac Watts, the "Joy to the World" hymn writer who believed that overloading one's head with information in a short period of time is not conducive to real learning: "As a Man may be eating all Day, and for want of Digestion is never nourish'd; so these endless Readers may cram themselves in vain with intellectual Food, and without real Improvement of their Minds, for want of digesting it by proper Reflections."

> 66 I can't believe we have our final exam on *Infinite Jest* tomorrow. I haven't even opened that book. Guess it's time to cram! 99

crash (verb | /kræʃ/):

To go to sleep; to stay over at a friend's house, either because you are too tired to venture back home or because Uber prices are surging and you can't stomach the thought of spending $53.69 for a two-minute drive.

Origin: Like many things in the 1960s, drugs were responsible for this word. According to some sources, *crash* formed in reference to hippies and how their bodies would "crash" after abusing certain illegal substances.

> **❝** Man, I had *way* too many Peeps tonight—I don't feel so great. Any chance I could crash at your place? **❞**

cray (adjective | /kreɪ/):

Crazy; delusional; an enduring nickname for *crayfish*.

Origin: Cray made its debut on the internet in 2001, when a user named "Jeremy from Chicago, IL" submitted an entry for it in an online slang dictionary. Over time, the word began creeping into the world's lexicon, eventually landing in a 2011 Kanye West/Jay-Z song and, later, the mouth of every teenager.

> **❝** Ketchup-flavored potato chips? That's cray. **❞**

crib (noun | /krɪb/):

Both "one's home" and "a cage for babies."

Origin: Shakespeare strikes again. The famed poet was the first to use this word, writing in *Henry IV, Part 2*: "Why rather sleepe liest thou in smoaky cribbes, . . . Then in the perfumde chambers of the great . . ." This idea of a "small smokey space" lent the word a negative connotation that latched onto its evolving definitions; over the next few decades, crib would come to mean anything from a brothel to a thief's target to an illegal Prohibition-era saloon. It wasn't until after WWII that the word reverted back to its original "tiny dwelling" meaning and reentered the English language as an acceptable synonym for "home."

> **❝** Hi, MTV! I'm a toddler and welcome to my crib! **❞**

AFTER THE BREAK:
SEE WHAT'S IN THEIR FRIDGE!!!

crunk (adjective | /krəŋk/):

Excited or full of energy, but not in the I-just-drank-three-energy-drinks-and-I-can-hear-my-heartbeat kind of way.

Origin: Likely derived from the past tense of the Southern phrase "to crank up" meaning "to party." *Crunk* made a resurgence in the 1990s thanks to the hip-hop community, who dropped the adjective into many of their hit songs. Don't ask me which ones.

> 66 All right, I've got my boom box, my shades, and my mocha frappucino with whip. I'm ready to get crunk. 99

crush (verb / noun | /krəʃ/):

To have short-lived romantic feelings for a peer, friend, celebrity, or English teacher; the object of such affections.

Origin: Isabella Maud Rittenhouse was a writer, teacher, and schoolgirl who kept a diary of her life in a small Illinois town during the early 1900s. In it, she describes someone weeping because "her crush is gone," which is the first time the word was used in the infatuation sense. Eric Partridge, a lexicographer with a passion for slang, suggested that the term may have formed from the word *mash*, a popular 1870s shorthand for "flirtatious behavior" and the name of a hit sitcom that wouldn't air for another 100 years.

> 66 I've Snapchatted my crush 203 times, and she hasn't opened any of them. Do you think she's playing hard to get? 99

daddy-o (noun | /ˈdædiˌoʊ/):

A cool dude, one who is probably not your actual dad.

Origin: *Daddy-o* (sometimes written as *daddio*) was a term of endearment used primarily by beatniks and jazz musicians during the 1950s to refer to other respectable adult males.

> ❝ Hey-o, daddy-o. Are you ready to make some sick music today? ❞

dank (adjective | /dæŋk/):

In regular use, dank means "unpleasantly moist." In slang use, it means "excellent" or "cool." How did those two wildly different definitions come to coexist? Keep reading . . .

Origin: Ninety-nine percent of the time, *dank* is a negative descriptor that brings to mind darkened caves reeking of mildew and death. But there is one tiny exception: weed. Marijuana plants grow exceedingly well in cold, wet, "dank" environments, leading many to draw connections between the word *dank* and something that is "good" or "high quality."

> ❝ Those are some dank loafers. ❞

dead (noun | /dɛd/):

A happy state of mind triggered by a funny or exciting event, as in "Oh my God, he was the father?! I'm dead."

Origin: This noun appeared on internet message boards back in the early 2000s as an exaggerated response to a joke or meme, similar to LOL, LMAO, and ROTFLCOPTER. In line with meme trends at the time that shortened or purposefully misspelled words to enhance their humor ("luk at the smol doggo"), *dead* was often written as *ded* or *I'm dying*, which did not cause as many concerned 911 calls as one might expect.

> ❝ Oh my God, that was hilarious. I'm dead. Ded. Deceased. Truly dying. Like, rolling over in my grave. Rotting away second by second. Literally talking to you from the ghost realm. Dead. ❞

dibs (noun | /dɪbz/):

A claim on someone or something, like an attractive boy or the one remaining bed in your childhood home that all seven siblings must fight over during the holidays. Usually yelled and accompanied by frantic pointing and waving.

Origin: *Dibs* is an American expression, but there seems to be no record of the word in the United States before 1932, when it burst onto the scene fully formed. However, it did appear much earlier in the United Kingdom in the form of *dibstones*—an ancient rock game similar to jacks in which one throws a ball and tries to grab (or perhaps "claim") pebbles while it's mid-bounce.

    " Our Yankee Swap is about to start, but you should all know that I have dibs on that electric razor, so paws off. "

diddly-squat (noun | /ˈdɪdliˌskwɔt/):

Something that is meaningless, like long division or poems written by two-year-olds.

Origin: *The Random House Historical Dictionary of American Slang* indicates that *diddly-squat* was born from *doodly-squat*, which mysteriously appeared in the 1930s and was replaced by *diddly-squat* in the 1970s. How? Unknown, so this whole etymology is diddly-squat.

    " Well gosh dangit, you think you know everything, and then one day you read some Twitter post and realize you know diddly-squat. "

dip (verb | /dɪp/):

"Let's dip." You've heard it before, probably from the mouth of the local Cool Boy the second he decides that the party he's at doesn't have enough hard seltzer or bouncy houses or whatever the kids are into these days.

Origin: Literally, no one knows. There's an abundance of theories, including one that says *dip* came from dips in the ground that remove people from view (just like leaving removes people from . . . wherever they were) and another that says it originated in hip-hop circles along with *bounce*, *boogie*, and *swayze*.

66 Let's make like chips and dip. 99

diss (verb | /dɪs/):

To say something insulting, like "Your cat's Instagram page is boring" or "You look like a lukewarm slice of ham."

Origin: Borrowed from Jamaica, along with reggae music and Bob Marley.

66 Mariah Carey dropped a sick diss track this morning to the tune of 'All I Want for Christmas' and it's baller. 99

divey (adjective | /ˈdaɪvi/):

Dark, shabby, and a little bit dangerous describes both your sister's questionable new boyfriend and "divey" locations (i.e., rundown bars, restaurants that host slam poetry nights in their smoky basements, etc.). Not all "divey" places are bad. In fact, charm is often the key to making them successful, as it's the only thing that offsets a dive's natural murder-y vibe.

Origin: The term *dive bar* actually appeared back in the late 1800s to describe drinking dens that "frequenters may 'dive' into without observation." As these locales became more common, so too did the adjective to describe them; by 1952, *divey* had entered common use.

66 That bar is so divey. The only people I see go in there are rowdy frat boys, Bon Jovi cover bands, and aspiring spoken word artists. 99

DM (verb / noun | /diɛm/):

Pronounced like "carpe *diem*," DM is an acronym for Direct Message—a private correspondence conducted over social media sites like Twitter. If someone has "slid into your DMs," it means they have messaged you individually, either to degrade your personal and political views, ask you on a date, or, if they're particularly delusional, both.

Origin: Messaging services have been around for years, but DMs didn't appear until 2018 when Twitter released the feature. Since then, many women have had to endure intrusive DMs asking about their relationship status and/or why they hate *The Big Lebowski.*

66 DM me your Social Security information, and I'll wire you one million dollars! 99

doggo (noun | /ˈdɔgoʊ/):

A dog. Also known in some circles as man's best friend, a pupper, or "my itty-bitty fur baby."

Origin: Dubbed one of the top 100 memes of the 2010s, *doggo* emerged during the nineteenth century as a verb for "to remain hidden" or "to lie flat." The dictionary speculates that the noun *doggo* may formed from there, perhaps as a twist on "the light sleep of dogs." Though the hard-boiled detective novels of the 1920s seized this word, it didn't gain mainstream recognition until 2016, when the popular We Rate Dogs Twitter account began flinging this nickname left and right.

❝Who's a good doggo? Is it you? Is it? IS IT?!❞

dollface (noun | /daɪfeɪs/):

A pretty girl who looks like a doll, but not the creepy killer kind.

Origin: First mentioned by Alfred Tennyson in 1884 ("A doll-face blanc'd and bloodless . . ."), this moniker refers to women whose faces are smooth, unblemished, or childlike. Though it sounds like a compliment, it's often used by older men in a misogynistic I-can-call-you-a-toy-and-get-away-with-it sort of way.

❝What's shaking, dollface? Who let you out of your dollhouse, hm?❞

done (adjective | /dən/):

Emotionally exhausted and often said with a look of exasperation after a long day or hearing a particularly dumb comment.

Origin: Likely birthed from the phrase "Stick a fork in me, I'm done." This frustrated remark rose to fame during the late 2000s.

> 66 You really think that two plus two is seven? Really? I'm . . . I'm so done. 99

dough (noun | /doʊ/):

Similar to *rocks*, *bill*, and *Jeffersons*, *dough* refers to money, and a lot of it.

Origin: You know how your dad would say, "Someone's gotta bring home the bread!" with a shrug, like you, a child, were supposed to know that bread equals rent? Well, in a backward way, *dough* formed from *bread*. When the term appeared sometime in the nineteenth century, owning bread was a sign of wealth; if you could afford food, specifically bread, which was a staple of people's diets at the time, then you probably had money to support yourself. Somewhere along the way, someone who thought they were clever baked up a new, similar nickname: *dough*.

> 66 Dude, you're three weeks behind on rent. Cough up the dough or I'll have you sleeping with the fishes. 99

downer (noun | /ˈdaʊnər/):

Someone who is overly negative and who always says things like "Well, don't you think the sky is *too* blue?" or "Sure, the McFlurry *looks* good, but have you noticed the calorie count? Do you want to have a heart attack at twenty-three?"

Origin: Although *downer* has been around since the 1970s (and likely referred to depressants and other drugs that were emerging), the jab really took off in 2004 when comedian Rachel Dratch unveiled her character Debbie Downer on the hit NBC variety show *Saturday Night Live!* Since that fateful evening, it has become a catchall term for anyone who's constantly looking for reasons to hate the universe.

" First name, Debbie. Last name, Downer. It's pretty boring, I know. "

drag (verb | /dræg/):

To roast someone by "dragging" them down with comments like "Did you fall into a dumpster this morning or is that your cologne?" or "I see you let your blind aunt choose your outfit again."

Origin: Though entries for "dragging" date back to 2011, it didn't gain steam until the late 2010s with the rise of Twitter—the platform best known for angry attacks from internet stars and now presidents.

" He cheated on you and he doesn't like cats? *Drag him.* "

dreamboat (noun | /ˈdrim̩bo͝ot/):

A hottie with a body. Can include celebrities, athletes, or your twelfth grade English teacher with the low voice and passion for poetry.

Origin: The *Oxford English Dictionary* marks the first appearance of this word in 1941, but other sources suggest it may have surfaced earlier. In fact, musicians Cliff Friend and Dave Franklin wrote a whole song about a dreamboat coming home in 1936, proving that seaward hunks have been riding the waves of our hearts since the early days of this country.

> **"** Mr. Dudley is *such* a dreamboat. Just look at that chinstrap beard and striped sweater vest. **"**

dump (verb | /dəmp/):

To end a relationship with someone, either because they cheated on you or you fell out of love with them or they accidentally stepped on your prize hamster while you were away at work.

Origin: *Dump*'s other literal meaning, "to drop something suddenly," likely spawned this figurative one, as "dumping someone" often entails leaving them suddenly and with no warning, causing them to run back to their friends with tears in their eyes, snot in their nose, and words like "no one will ever love me again" in their mouths.

> **"** Bad relationship giving you the blues? Call 1-800-DUMPHIM and I'll dump your toxic boyfriend for you! **"**

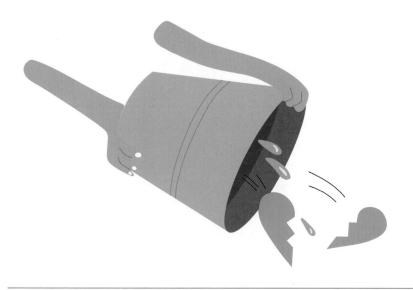

dutch (verb | /dətʃ/):

When a date offers to "go dutch," what they're really saying is "as much as I want to be chivalrous and buy both of our breakfasts, I have just enough money in my bank account for my sesame bagel (plus tax) but I don't want you to know that, so I'm going to use this cutesy offer as a way to pivot away from a conversation about my finances."

Back in the seventeenth century, England and the Netherlands were known to bicker over their trade routes. Their consistently stingy agreements earned the latter country a selfish reputation, one that helped give rise to this helpful phrase.

❝❝I know I got the filet mignon and the top-shelf scotch, and you just got a Coke, but do you want to go dutch on this bill?**❞❞**

dweeb (noun | /dwib/):

A person who is both a dork and a loser. A double whammy!

Origin: The origin of *dweeb* is as mysterious as the dweeb your popular sister just brought home from prom. Which is to say, no one fully understands why it happened. The *Oxford English Dictionary* thinks it "probably" came from *dwarf* mixed with *feeb* as in *feeble*, but other sources think it was a slang word of either the 1960s or the '80s. Ask your nearest Gen Xer for confirmation.

❝❝Don't be a dweeb, Daryl. Eat the bug or go home.**❞❞**

egghead (noun | /ɛghɛd/):

An intellectual, the kind you might mock by calling them an "intellectual" with air quotes, as if their Harvard education means nothing to you.

Origin: Like most terrible things, *egghead* was a product of American politics. Even worse, it attributes its popularity to Richard Nixon, who used the word to describe his party's opponent in the 1952 presidential election. Fed up with the "intellectuals" who headed the Democratic party, Republicans at the time were desperate for a biting insult for these figures who they deemed elitist. As a nod to Democratic candidate Adlai Stevenson's balding head, Nixon conjured the word *egghead* and slung it around numerous times in that year's election cycle. Apparently, it worked: Dwight D. Eisenhower and Richard Nixon had the winning ticket that year.

66 Humpty Dumpty was the worst. Not only was he a klutz, but he could not stop talking about his Yale degree. What an egghead. 99

epic (adjective | /ˈɛpɪk/):

Simply amazing, like the backflip your buddy just did into the pool or the belly flop that he did when he hit the water.

Origin: Once used to describe long, heroic stories with knights and dragons, *epic* is now mostly used to describe YouTube videos your little brother watched the other day. Its use as an adjective to describe extraordinary things, though, likely formed from this original definition, as "fantastic stories" eventually whittled down to "fantastic." At the turn of the twenty-first century, the word *epic* once again moved in a new direction with the coining of the phrase "epic fail," or a mistake so incredible, it's worthy of its own fantasy epic.

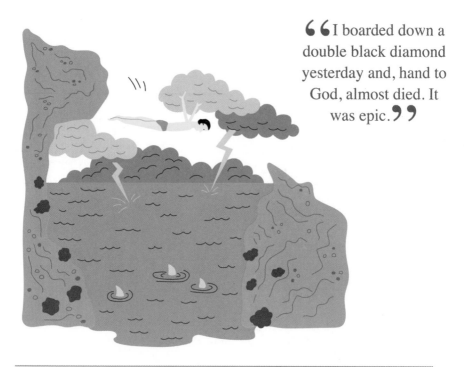

❝ I boarded down a double black diamond yesterday and, hand to God, almost died. It was epic. ❞

extra (adjective | /ˈɛkstrə/):

Over the top, dramatic, or incredibly enthusiastic. Your sister who hired a professional photographer to take her Facebook profile picture is extra. Your mom who made a photo album of her favorite Snapchat selfies is extra. Your grandpa who bought a seventy-two-inch screen to play Solitaire on is extra. There are a lot of ways to be extra.

Origin: With roots in Latin, *extra* is most well known as an abbreviated form of *extraordinary*, which makes sense considering someone who is "extra" is generally doing something "extra-ordinary" or beyond ordinary. The word didn't catch on as a slang term, though, until around 2017 with the appearance of the Salt Bae meme, featuring a man in a tight white shirt and sunglasses sprinkling salt onto a steak with more flair than the country's entire teenage population. Since then, youths have strived to be as "extra" as that mysterious Turkish man.

> **"** Did you really live-tweet the livestream of your Dad's wedding? That's so extra. **"**

facepalm (verb / noun | /ˈfeɪsˌpɑː(l)m/):

To drop one's face into the palm of one's hand, often as a dramatic or exasperated response to something stupid a boy did.

Origin: Though *facepalm* has been recorded as early as 1996, the term didn't take off until the 2000s with the explosion of internet culture and memes. One of the first recorded instances of this word, for example, was on a 2001 message board, when one user made this geeky HTML joke: <facepalm>doh!<facepalm>. But it wasn't until 2008, with the sudden introduction of the Patrick Stewart face-in-palm *Star Trek* meme, that this verb stole our hearts and our hands.

66 When David tried to ice skate on our frozen swimming pool and then fell in, all I could do was facepalm. 99

fam (noun | /fæm/):

An abbreviated word for "family" lovingly used to describe any group of people that one might consider, well, their family, whether that's the ragtag group of kids that you hang around with during theater practice, the coworkers who make your nine-to-five job feel like home, or the arctic wolves that adopted you as an infant and raised you as one of their own.

Origin: An early 2000s colloquialism that first appeared in the 2003 hip-hop song "This Is What I Do" by The Diplomats, who sang "And that's my word fam, I swore to my mother I'd get you. Made a phone call, now I'm done with the issue."

> **"Let's go, fam. The trailer's fired up and Walley World is waiting!"**

fartknocker (noun | /fartˈnɑkər/):

Someone you don't want to hang out with, either because they're toxic, annoying, or likely to tank your social status if you're seen standing near them.

Origin: Historically a derogatory term, *fartknocker* reentered our vernacular thanks to the 1990s cartoon *Beavis and Butthead*, in which the lead characters often tossed out insults like "turd-burglar," "bunghole," and other terms any second-grader would admire.

> **"Hey, fartknocker, didn't I tell you to stay away from my treehouse? Beat it."**

finesse (verb | /fɪˈnɛs/):

To expertly diffuse a difficult or high-stress situation in hopes of achieving a particular (and often self-serving) goal. Can either be done through diplomacy or with a swift smack to the back of the head.

Origin: From the French word of the same name meaning "subtlety in action," *finesse* is believed to have originated in Chicago, where it grew and eventually took hold of the music scene. During the 2010s, it appeared in everything from "China Town" by Migos to "Finesse" by Bruno Mars. Though it can also mean "to smooth out a problem," in these circumstances, it usually means "to convince someone to do something that I want to do."

> **❝** I spent five hundred dollars on wine the other day in hopes of finessing my lady into a fancy night in . . . but she insisted on going out on the town anyway. **❞**

finna (verb | /ˈfɪnnə/):

A synonym for "going to" that looks like the name for a young Swedish girl. Isn't that right, Finna?

Origin: Strangely not the result of a typo, *finna* actually found its roots in African American Vernacular English (AAVE). It comes from the classic Southern phrase "fixing to," which eventually morphed into "finna," replacing "gonna" as the American teenager's favorite shorthand for "going to."

finsta (noun | /ˈfɪnˌstɑ/):

A rinsta ("real Insta") is an Instagram account where you post curated, wholesome pictures of yourself volunteering or reading books by the beach so that your parents think you're the pure, hardworking kid that they brag to your relatives about and not the wild party animal that your finsta ("fake Insta") suggests.

Origin: A portmanteau of *fake* and *Instagram*, finstas are private accounts that teens use to post unfiltered content that they feel like they can't share on their real Instagram account, either because it's lewd, illegal, or uncool. The term first appeared online in 2011 and snowballed into one of the hottest words of the era, inspiring memes and a slew of (real) headlines like "What's a finsta and does your teen have one?" and "Ditch your therapist, make a finsta."

❝Did you see my finsta post the other day? No, not my rinsta. Nope, not the dinsta either. Nah, that was on my shinsta. Keep up, Pops.❞

fire (adjective | /ˈfaɪ(ə)r/):

Very impressive, like a delicious meal or a Monopoly game that doesn't end in an all-out family war.

Origin: In 2010, the fire emoji was officially released into the world, launching an era of slang centered around the theme of heat (hot, roast, flaming, etc.). *Fire* was one such word, rising alongside phrases like "it's lit" and Snapchat "streaks" represented by the fire icon.

❝ That acai bowl from the breakfast hut down the street? It's fire. ❞

fit (adjective / noun | /fɪt/):

Fit can either mean a good-looking outfit ("That's a nice fit you got there!") or simply good-looking ("That's a nice, fit face you got there!").

Origin: A favorite activity of teens these days is shortening words that don't need to be shortened, and *fit* is the prime example. This abbreviation popped up on the internet around 2001, but didn't make its mark until 2016.

fleek (adjective | /flik/):

Spot on, like "that geek is on fleek."

Origin: In 2014, Vine user Peaches Monroee posted a video where she described her eyebrows as "on fleek" (read: on point) and her little minions spread the word, launching it into the popular vernacular.

❝ Girl, your face is on fleek today. ❞

flex (verb / noun | /flɛks/):

To show off or something one uses to show off, like a fancy car or an Instagram account with a six-figure following.

Origin: People have been gloating since the beginning of time, but people have only been "flexing" since 2014, when twenty-one-year-old rapper Rae Sremmurd released his hip-hop song "No Flex Zone," which proposed "flex-free" spaces dedicated to being yourself and not bragging for, like, two seconds, *please*.

floss (verb | /flas/):

To show off one's assets, like a person flossing their teeth, flashing their pearly whites for the whole world to see. Can also refer to the mega popular dance move where one moves their arms and hips in opposite directions to create the appearance, almost, that they're flossing their body.

Origin: The *Oxford English Dictionary* tracks the first use of this definition to Robin Hyde's 1938 novel *The Godwits Fly*. In it, one of the characters advises another not to "go flossing around girls." Thought to be a product of the African American community, *flossing* quickly went on to become a staple of English slang. In 2016, it developed a new meaning after videos of American teenager Russell Horning doing the dance move described above went viral.

> ❝ You trying to floss, bro?
> Because this is a flex-free zone. ❞

fly (adjective | /flaɪ/):

Good-looking or unflappable. Not the insect that zooms by your ear in the middle of the night, waking you up in a cold sweat and wishing you'd closed the window a few hours ago like you were supposed to.

Origin: In the early nineteenth century, *fly* surfaced as an adjective for "sharp," "nimble," or "in the know," often being used by gangsters in the criminal underworld to describe guys that were well-informed of their city's happenings. This "in the know" meaning expanded to "generally smart" and eventually "cool or attractive." At least, that's what some scholars think. Others wonder if it was inspired by a fruit fly's inability to be caught off guard, leading to the suggestion that "fly guys" were slick and did things effortlessly.

FOMO (noun | /foʊmoʊ/):

The very distinct fear that somewhere out there, someone is doing something fun without you, so you need to get up off the couch, get dressed, and join them, or risk seeing the Instagrams of it later in the day and feeling like you missed out on a really important life memory and/or photo op.

Origin: Though technically an acronym, FOMO has become sort of its own standalone term for the sinking feeling you get in your stomach when you see that your friend group organized a Secret Santa swap without you. It often prompts questions like "Why didn't they ask me?" or "Was my gift last year not good enough?" or "I thought Connor wanted a weight loss powder!?" The nickname FOMO was coined by Harvard student Patrick McGinnis back in 2004 to describe his friend group's existential need to "live life to the fullest" following the rattling days of 9/11, and the anxiety that came with that mantra. They dubbed the feeling Fear of a Better Option, or FOBO, which eventually became FOMO: Fear of Missing Out.

foxy (adjective | /ˈfɑksi/):

When someone says "you're foxy," they're not saying that you resemble the popular carnivorous species native to Western Europe. They're calling you attractive, so the appropriate response would be "Thank you!" or "Sir, please leave me alone." Whatever feels right for the situation.

Origin: Back in the medieval days, an unnamed writer complaining about fashion remarked on his disdain for women's clothing that was often so tight, women had to stuff foxtails in their pants to prevent their clothes from being totally see-through . . . thus attracting even more attention to that area. Somehow, this flirtatious meaning survived up until the 1970s, when it came back to life to describe sexy, fur-wearing ladies of that era.

> **"** You're looking awfully foxy today, and not because of the massive tail you have draped around your shoulders. **"**

freal (adverb | /fri(ə)l/):

Seriously. No, seriously. *Freal* is a contraction of "for real" which means "technically, seriously."

Origin: According to Urban Dictionary, *freal* (or *freals*) surfaced around 2003 as a response to any piece of information that was surprising, like "You got front row tickets to see Shia Labeouf recite the phone book in the nude? Freal?"

> **"** Yeah, dude. Shia claims he's trying to prove that there's meaning in every medium, even phone books. It's gonna be epic, freal. **"**

friendzone (verb / noun | /frɛndzoʊn/):

To establish a platonic relationship with someone who is interested in you romantically by pointedly using words like *buddy* and *pal*.

Origin: Could it *be* any more obvious? The 1994 sitcom *Friends* popularized this term in the season 1 episode "The One with the Blackout," in which Joey tells Ross he has no chance with Rachel because she has delegated him to "the friendzone."

> **"** Things were going really well, until she pinched my cheeks and called me her 'precious little bud.' I've definitely been friendzoned. **"**

fro-yo (noun | /ˈfroʊ ˌjoʊ/):

You know in science fiction movies where the alien takes the form of the protagonist's mother and tries to convince them that they are the real Cheryl? That's what fro-yo, or "frozen yogurt," is: it looks like ice cream, feels like ice cream, and vaguely tastes like ice cream—but deep down isn't really ice cream.

Origin: Fro-yo was created in the 1970s by New England company H. P. Hood, who marketed the product as Frogurt. By the 2000s, this healthy alternative to ice cream had gone from "cute trend" to "available on every street corner in America."

❝I'm on this new 'no carb, no sugar, no joy' diet where I primarily eat bananas and fro-yo. I've lost 20 pounds and my vision, so I'd say it's going all right!❞

fuzz (noun | /fəz/):

The nicest derogatory term for police that you'll ever hear.

Origin: In the 1960s and '70s, members of the Metropolitan Police in England wore thick black uniforms and helmets covered in felt, causing the British (and later groovy Americans) to call them "fuzz."

❝We can't do our robbery as planned. The local doughnut shop is closed today, so the fuzz are everywhere.❞

gassed (verb / adjective | /gæst/):

It can mean to compliment someone excessively to boost their ego, to be overtly drunk, or to simply be exhausted.

Origin: While *gassed* as an adjective for *drunk* has been around since 1863, the verb "to gas" has only been around since the late 2000s, ever since Drake dropped the phrase in his 2009 song "Money to Blow." Since then, people have used it as a way to demand praise from friends in times of distress, like after a bad date or on a oh-my-God-I-can't-leave-the-house-with-this-haircut day.

> **"**I just found out Carl is cheating on me with my mother and I'm distraught. Gas me up, ladies.**"**

geezer (noun | /ˈgizər/):

An old man who is eccentric and out of touch with society, either because he doesn't know how to work an iPhone or because he still thinks that Dippin' Dots are the future of ice cream.

Origin: When it appeared in the 1800s, *geezer* (from the English dialectical word *guiser*, for "one who dresses up in disguise") referred to men of any age who were considered odd (perhaps as if they were masquerading as someone else, in reference to its original *guiser* meaning) or unpleasant. It wasn't until the 1920s that age became factored into the definition, for reasons unknown.

> **"**Stop getting your news from Facebook, you old geezer!**"**

ghost (verb | /goʊst/):

There are two types of ghosting. The first kind, regular ghosting, happens when the person you started casually dating after a promising Tinder date three months ago suddenly stops responding to your messages, as if they have died and become a ghost. The second kind, soft ghosting, occurs when said person slowly cuts off communication, responding to texts with a simple "like" or ignoring all of your messages but watching every single one of your Insta stories. The only thing worse than ghosting is *literally* being haunted by a ghost (and even that feels better, because at least ghosts are straightforward about what they want from you).

Origin: Though the noun *ghost* has been around for centuries, the verb *ghost* only appeared in the late 2000s to describe the slow, intentional fizzling of relationships. Mainstream news caught onto the phenomena after Charlize Theron publicly admitted to ghosting Sean Penn toward the end of their relationship, proving that yes, celebrities *are* just like us!

66 Casper was a friendly ghost, until he canceled our date night and began soft ghosting me around the holidays. 99

glow (noun | /gloʊ/):

When paired with *up* (as in *glow up*) this noun has a transformative meaning: a positive change in appearance. It's usually said in excitement after a trip to the salon or after seeing embarrassing photos of yourself from a decade ago.

Origin: Sometimes stylized as *glo up* or *glow-up*, *glow up* seems to be a spin on *grow up*, as in "I've grown up a lot since high school." This became clear in 2018 when a social media trend titled #2012vs2018 challenged users to post photos of them from both years to illustrate how well they've aged, leading to another hashtag: #GloUpChallenge.

> **❝ Oh my God, Mia. Who knew becoming a princess would lead to such a glow up? ❞**

gnarly (adjective | /ˈnɑrli/):

Distressing or dangerous, like your anxious mother or the seventy-foot-tall tidal wave about to engulf you. Eventually, this definition morphed, changing from "disturbing" to "excellent."

Origin: A staple of surfer culture in 1970s America, *gnarly* came from the ancient word *gnarled* meaning "twisted" or "rugged." From there, it came to describe waves with those qualities, which were often the most dangerous due to their sheer size and strength. While most people would be afraid of these monster waves (hence, the "dangerous" part of the definition), surfers became fascinated by them, causing the word to take on a more positive meaning.

> **❝ Doctors said I was legally dead for at least a minute after my surfing accident, but I'd ride that wave again if I could. It was gnarly. ❞**

goals (noun | /goʊls/):

Accomplishments that one aspires to have, including friends ("squad goals"), relationships ("couple goals"), physique ("body goals"), or the like. Usually accompanied by a hashtag and an aesthetically pleasing Instagram post, *goals* can be applied to almost anything. See a cute puppy on the street? #PetGoals. Catch the table next to you at lunch chowing down on a glistening steak? #FoodGoals. Find a picture in a doctor's office of a healthy pink brain? #OrganGoals.

Origin: Squads have been present in hip-hop culture for years, but in 2015, Taylor Swift began captioning many of her tour photos with #SquadGoals, launching a new phrase for "a desireable female friend group." This *goals* phenomena didn't stop there; many began to latch the term onto anything or anyone they admired.

❝Michelle Obama is #MomGoals, right ladies?❞

GOAT (noun | /goʊt/):

An acronym for Greatest of All Time. Your Patriots fan friend has used it in reference to Tom Brady, and honestly, they're right.

Origin: Muhammad Ali was known for many things, and GOAT was, apparently, one of them. The famous boxer frequently referred to himself as "the greatest of all time," bringing the phrase into the public eye and cementing it in sporting history. His wife even went on to launch a company under the name G.O.A.T. to house all of the boxer's intellectual properties. But despite all of that, the standalone term GOAT did not break into the dictionary until 2018—a year after the Patriots stunning comeback at the 2017 Super Bowl, during which there was a spike in hashtags linking the team's quarterback Tom Brady and the celebratory acronym.

gobbledygook (noun | /ˈɡabəldiˌɡuk/):

A Snuggles smooch red tabletop baseball yippersnapper mouse watch. Didn't catch that? Probably because it was a load of gobbledygook, or nonsense.

Origin: First used by Texas politician Maury Maverick in a 1944 memo chastising politicians for using long-winded, pretentious "gobbledygook language." When asked how he came up with the word, he admitted that he borrowed it from the imitative sound of turkeys.

golddigger (noun | /ˈɡoʊl(d)ˌdɪɡər/):

Someone who digs for gold, either in riverbanks in the Midwest or in the pockets of a lucrative and unsuspecting business owner.

Origin: First mentioned in Rex Beach's 1911 book *The Ne'er-Do-Well*, the term took off in 1919 after the release of the play *The Gold Diggers*, which featured showgirls singing about rich men and their desire to marry them for their money. This association between the term and women runs deep, as it was well known that low-class women were expected to wed wealthy men in order to increase their socioeconomic status, also called "marrying up." Sorry, boys.

66 Now, I ain't saying she's a golddigger, but she did ask me for my bank information on our second date, so it's entirely possible. 99

grandstand (verb | /ˈgræn(d)ˌstænd/):

To speak or behave in a particular way in order to attract positive public attention. It's what your sister does when she announces to the family that she's going to do everyone's laundry, out of the goodness of her heart and *definitely* not to prove that she's the better child.

Origin: This word was tossed out by college baseball players in the 1890s in reference to "grandstand plays," or unnecessary plays involving a lot of theatrics. Unsurprisingly, the word eventually made its way into politics and has stayed there ever since.

      ❝ Quit your grandstanding, Eric; we all know you're not going to put free vending machines in the cafeteria. ❞

gravy (adjective | /ˈgreɪvi/):

Excellent. Yes, Grandpa, like the food.

Origin: There's an Old English saying, "It's all gravy!" that suggests that life is made up of the basics—meat and potatoes—and anything extra is gravy. As a result, gravy came to stand for anything considered excellent or a bonus. It's in this way that gravy also came to symbolize luxuries like money.

    ❝ You've gone vegan, huh? Well that's just gravy. I'll get all the turkey on Thanksgiving! ❞

greaseball (noun | /grisbal/):

A derogatory name for a person (or group of people) who were unpopular or gross. Not the name of a slippery ball game, but if anyone would like to invent one, the opportunity is there.

Origin: The etymology for this one is, unfortunately, not the best. It originated around the 1930s as a moniker for Italian Americans who were stereotyped as having thick, oily black hair. It eventually came to represent anyone who was generally slimy.

> ❝ I accidentally touched Stephen's hair the other day, and my hand came back dripping wet. He's such a greaseball. ❞

greaser (noun | /ˈgrisər/):

A tough guy who is as slick as the hair products that he soaks his 'fro in.

Origin: Though the term originated in the nineteenth century as a pejorative nickname for lower-class workers, its association with the tall, dark, and handsome greasers didn't emerge until the late 1950s, when disillusioned post-WWII youth sought ways to rebel against the picture-perfect boomer lifestyle that all millennials would eventually come to resent.

> ❝ Hey, hot stuff. Are you one of those greaser types or is it raining outside? Your hair's looking pretty wet . . . ❞

grifter (noun | /ˈɡrɪftər/):

A con artist so good that you're usually thanking them as they walk out the door with your money and Social Security number.

Origin: Likely a combination of *graft* (i.e., to earn a profit by shady means) and *drifter* (someone who wanders from place to place), *grifter* perfectly encapsulates both of its roots, as the criminals it describes are often nomads, traveling from city to city swindling just enough people just to get by. It emerged during the early days of the American circus in 1906, when "confidence tricksters" were a form of entertainment and not an illegal activity.

> ❝ That grifter stole my AirPods! There were right there in my pocket, and now they're—oh wait, I found them. ❞

grind (noun | /ɡraɪnd/):

A period of hard, steady work. People that are "on the grind" include students, working-class parents, and "influencers" in Los Angeles who are desperately trying to hit one hundred thousand TikTok followers.

Origin: Invented by none other than college students in 1851, *grind* was originally described as "a very long lesson which they are required to learn," which feels like the exact complaint you'd expect to hear from a college student.

> ❝ My boss has thrown three staplers at my head today but hey, that's part of the grind. You just gotta push through and—oh, here comes another one. Duck! ❞

grindage (noun | /ɡraɪndɪdʒ/):

A plate of delicious food. It's what Instagrams are made of.

Origin: This 1980s and '90s gem came from the mouth of Gen Xers and later from the mouth of Pauly Shore in the 1992 comedy *Encino Man*, and then again in the 1993 classic *Son in Law*. If you've ever wondered where the "munchin' on my grindage" meme came from, now you know.

❝Wanna hit up DQ for some sick grindage?❞

grody (adjective | /ˈɡroʊdi/):

Disgusting or revolting. There's no such thing as "a little grody"; grody only exists on a large scale, hence the phrase "grody to the max."

Origin: Nineteen eighty-two saw the release of the song "Valley Girl" by Frank Zappa and his daughter Moon Zappa, which popularized a number of phrases including "gag me with a spoon" and, in this case, "grody to the max."

❝California girls are undeniable, but California boys . . . they're pretty grody.❞

groovy (adjective | /ˈgruvi/):

Spectacular with a splash of swagger. It was originally used to refer to upbeat jazz music and the talented musicians who performed it, the kind that slipped on stage effortlessly, like a needle sliding through the groove of a vinyl record.

Origin: Birthed from the American jazz culture of the 1920s, *groovy* once described music that had a "groove" or a rhythm, hence the use of the word *grooves* to mean "hot tunes." Popular culture welcomed this word with open arms, carrying it through the 1940s, '50s, '60s, and '70s. It has even managed to sneak into kids' shows like *Scooby-Doo*, which features a lanky guy named Shaggy Rogers (a kindred spirit of the hippie generation) who thought everything other than monsters was "groovy."

66 That's a groovy beat. Is that Carly Rae Jepsen? 99

G

gucci (adjective | /guˈtʃɪ/):

Acceptable or fine, like "Is it gucci for me to put my Gucci bag on the table? I try not to let it touch the ground. You know, because it's Gucci."

Origin: Unsurprisingly, the adjective form of *gucci* came from the bag brand of the same name. Gucci, a longtime staple of the fashion world, is known for its elegance and style. This reputation for excellence eventually became synonymous with the word *gucci* itself. Not to mention, its similarity to the word *good* makes swapping it out fairly simple (but also wildly confusing).

66 Is it gucci for me to use your toothbrush? I hope so, because I already did. 99

hang (verb | /hæŋ/):

To spend time with someone, even if that "time" consists of watching back-to-back cat documentaries.

Origin: Back in 1811, long before internet ads or commercials, business owners would hang out signs on poles near their place of work as a way to promote their goods. People would often gather around these hang outs (to, you know, read them), leading to any mingling group being called a "hangout."

> 66 Hey, do you want to hang later and stalk people on the internet? I've been thinking about that girl Paige from eighth grade, and I want to know if she's had any more babies. 99

hangry (adjective | /ˈhæŋgri/):

When your mother comes storming into the house after a twelve-hour day and whips open the refrigerator with a growl, she's hangry ("hungry" + "angry") and you should probably retreat to your room before you're chewed out.

Origin: *Hangry* wasn't dubbed an "official" dictionary word until 2018, but it existed long before that. Most sources point to Rebecca Camu's 1992 short story *A Splinter of Glass* as the first place to use the word, but the *Oxford English Dictionary* suggests that it dates as far back as 1918. No one is immune to hangry feelings—after all, it's biological. When you don't eat for a long period of time, your glucose levels drop, causing simple tasks like "reading" or "talking to someone without screaming" to feel impossible.

haunt (noun | /hɔnt/):

A popular hang-out spot. Doesn't have to be haunted by spirits, but could be.

Origin: The word itself is likely from the Old French word *hanter* ("to visit regularly"), though the ghostly sense ("to return to a place after one has died") didn't catch on until Shakespeare's use of the word in his 1590 play *A Midsummer Night's Dream*.

headdesk (verb / noun | /ˈhɛdˌdɛsk/):

To strike one's head against a desk repeatedly as a dramatic display of exasperation, or the act of doing so. Headdesk comes just after *facepalm* and before *bodyground* on the *ugh* scale.

Origin: A very 2000s word, *headdesk* naturally rose from the depths of internet forums, first appearing on a Usenet role-playing group in 2005.

> **❝** I've explained the dangers of capitalism to my five-year-old thrice, and he still asks me to buy him toys for Christmas. Headdesk. **❞**

heavy (adjective | /ˈhɛvi/):

Emotionally deep. Usually uttered in response to a dark confession that someone might have physically struggled to carry, like "I accidentally killed my gerbil" or "I prefer Pepsi over Coke."

Origin: In addition to being one of the most popular bands of all time, The Beatles also hold the distinction of popularizing this '60s-era word in their song "I Want You (She's So Heavy)" which consists of the boys singing variations of "I want you" twenty-four separate times.

> **❝** You haven't cried in fifty-three years? And you're fifty-four? Man, that's heavy. **❞**

high-key (adverb | /haɪki/):

Straight up. Different from *low-key* in that *high-key* exudes confidence and pride, while *low-key* implies a degree of secrecy. Like, when you low-key want something, you like it but not enough to tell your friends. But when you high-key want something, you will scream it from the rooftops and post about it on Facebook like a picture of a newborn baby.

Origin: Supposedly coined by rapper Styles P in a 2013 Young Roddy track (along with *low-key*), *high-key* didn't fully take off until Drake began dropping it in his own music.

> **❝** I high-key want your girlfriend, bro. **❞**

hip (adverb | /hɪp/):

Fashionable. What you wish the kids would call you.

Origin: Unknown. It's generally believed to have come from the African American jazz community of the 1930s and '40s, but no one knows exactly from where. Some say it's derived from an earlier word *hep*—while others say it's in reference to opium smokers who had to lie on their sides (or their hips) to consume the drug.

---

hippie (noun | /ˈhɪpi/):

A person belonging to the counterculture movement of the 1960s. Originating on college campuses during the Vietnam War, hippies were a symbol of the anti-war movement, representing groups of young people who were opposed to the violence happening overseas and looking for ways to express their unconventional dissent. This desire to rebel led to widespread use of hallucinogenic drugs, sexual fluidity, and flower crowns.

Origin: A play on the term *hip*, which emerged a few years earlier during the jazz age. As time went on and the country's counterculture movement began to grow, *hip* slowly became repurposed, first to describe groups of politically inclined and "in the know" teens (who garnered the name *hips*) and, later, the *hippys* or *hippies* of the Vietnam era.

❝ Mom was for sure a hippie in her younger years. She takes barefoot walks in the forest every morning, for God's sake. It's pretty obvious. ❞

hipster (noun | /ˈhɪpstər/):

A modern youth going against the grain. Like hippies, but with more beards and less drugs. Hipsters can often be found drinking out of glass mugs, wearing beanies, and carrying vinyl records of the latest local indie band. Basically, anything the rest of society might consider "different."

Origin: The 1930s word for jazz enthusiasts, *hepsters*, accidentally inspired this word, thanks to a typo in a New York review of Cab Calloways *Hepster's Dictionary* that resulted in the switching of the *e* with the *i*. The word's similarity to the word *hip* (meaning "cool") led to *hipster* adopting a similar meaning.

hitched (adjective | /hɪtʃt/):

Married quickly, probably in Vegas, probably while drunk, probably to a stranger named Candy whom you met in the line for Fat Tuesdays. You got the Blue Bayou. She got the Cat 5 Hurricane. A match made in slurpee heaven.

Origin: Just as horses get "hitched" to a wagon, humans get "hitched" to each other. At least, that's what the inventor of this word had in mind when they came up with it back in the 1500s.

> **❝** I'm three tequilas in and ready for love. You trying to get hitched, honey?**❞**

homie (noun | /ˈhoʊmi/):

A term of endearment for one's closest friends. Sometimes expressed as *home skillet* by middle schoolers and their AIM away messages.

Origin: Short for *homeboy* or *homegirl*, a 1970s classic.

❝ Nice seeing you, homie. Tell the fam I said hi. ❞

hooked (adjective | /hʊkt/):

Addicted. You can be "hooked on love," "hooked on drugs," or "hooked on Phonics." It's all the same feeling.

Origin: First appearing in 1925, *hooked* became a common way to describe drug users who became stuck on narcotics like a fish trapped on a hook.

❝ Have you seen that new TV show *Hooked* about the history of hooks? I'm hooked, lemme tell ya. ❞

hoosegow (noun | /ˈhusˌɡaʊ/):

Nobody puts baby in the corner, but somebody could put baby in the hoosegow if baby breaks the rules. That's because *hoosegow* is 1920s jargon for "prison," even though it sounds more like the noise an injured goose might make.

Origin: Taken from the Spanish word *juzgao* ("jail") which came from *juzgado* ("courtroom") due to the fact that these two places were often housed in the same building. It's often associated with cowboys, whose vocabulary was made up largely of Spanish words they'd mangled.

> ❝ Howdy, Earl. How was the hoosegow the second time around? As good as the first? ❞

horsefeathers (noun | /hɔ(ə)rsfɛðərs/):

An expletive similar to blasphemy but significantly goofier.

Origin: Sometimes written as two words, *horsefeathers* was coined by comic-strip artist William "Billy" de Beck around the late 1920s. He mentions the word in his *Barney Google* series, which features a man talking to his pet horse.

> ❝ Eva said she loves you? Horsefeathers. Eva only loves herself. And English breakfast tea. ❞

humblebrag (noun | /ˈhʌmb(ə)lbræg/):

Coined by the late comedy writer Harris Wittels in 2010 via a parody Twitter account, *humblebrag* refers to people who fake modesty by slipping brags into seemingly humble statements, like "Got super sweaty while rescuing orphans from a burning building this morning, how embarrassing!" or "The pen broke while I was signing the lease for my new condo and the ink got all over my hands, sad!"

Origin: Didn't we just talk about this?

> **❝** Sorry I'm late, I was delivering my third book to the publisher and totally lost track of time! I promise this is not a humblebrag. **❞**

humdinger (adjective / noun | /ˈˌhəmˈdɪŋgər/):

Remarkable; a real winner, someone you'd want to take home to Mom and Dad and your stepbrother Carl, who is twenty-six and refuses to move out of the house because he's determined to start his own graphic design company, even though he has no graphic design experience or relevant internships. But hey, what do you know, huh?

Origin: Contrary to popular internet rumors, *humdinger* was not named after Arnold Humdinger, the man who tried to land his plane on the tip of Mount Everest. Rather, it was most likely a mash-up of *hummer* and *dinger*, *hummer* meaning "something so fast or efficient that it hums along" and *dinger* meaning "anything in the superlative."

> **❝** You're a real humdinger, Mum, always making me sandwiches with the crusts cut off, just the way I like it. **❞**

hypebeast (noun | /haɪpbist/):

A trend chaser; someone who only likes things that have become mainstream or super popular. Think of the friend who starts listening to that indie song you showed them, but only after the song airs on the radio. They're a hypebeast (and they're also the worst).

Origin: A mix of *hype* (over-the-top encouragement) and *beast* (someone exceptionally skilled). At the peak of sneakerhead culture in the 1990s and 2000s, when snagging the latest shoe model became a bona fide hobby among many fashion-forward men, a college student named Kevin Ma launched a website called Hypebeast to document his latest sneaker finds. Soon, the blog had cemented the word's place in popular culture and sparked a wave of other *hypebeast* terms like *hypebae* ("a female hypebeast"), *to hypebeast* ("to act like a poser"), and *hypebeastiality* ("someone who is romantically interested in hypebeasts").

❝ Dude, I showed you *My Little Pony* like seven months ago and now, all of a sudden, your Fluttershy's 'biggest fan'? You're such a hypebeast. **❞**

THERE'S A NEW FAD?!

ice (noun | /aɪs/):

Jewelry. Specifically, diamonds. You know, those tiny rocks on top of rings that you spend twenty grand on, only to have it thrown back at you ten years later after your marriage has crumbled, along with your self-esteem.

Origin: In the 1920s, mobsters like Al Capone used the word *ice* to describe diamonds that he and his cronies would peddle around the city. As the Roaring Twenties began to take off, soon, too, did the need for ostentatious clothing to match the swanky style that the era demanded. And so came the rise of wearable bling or ice.

❝ That's a sweet chunk of ice on your finger, madam. Did he go to Jared's? ❞

ink-slinger (noun | /ɪŋkˈslɪŋə/):

A journalist; a tattoo artist; a writer of low-quality content like pulp fiction, erotica, or anything else your Aunt May deems "not sophisticated enough" for her monthly book club.

Origin: Appeared in the mid-nineteenth century as a play on *gunslinger*, if I had to guess.

❝ Those ink-slingers at the New York Times have been writing terribly mean words about me all day. Can I sue them, Daddy? ❞

jam (verb / noun | /dʒæm/):

To play music together, often in your parents' basement, eliciting complaints to the tune of "you're a grown man, Jason, if you need somewhere to do band practice, how about you move into your own place?"

Origin: The *Oxford English Dictionary* suggests the "shove into a small space" meaning of *jam* is onomatopoeic and appeared back in the eighteenth century. This idea of "wedging" into a space led to the association between *jam* and tight or pressure-filled situations (traffic jams, gun jam, etc.). It's also where the notion of edible jam came from, as this sweet food is made by crushing berries into a spreadable paste. Where exactly music came into the picture, though, is unclear. Some think "jam sessions" (where musicians would get together to play for fun) were inspired by the tasty condiment, as if playing music was a "treat" like the food itself.

> **❝** I finally got that electric guitar that I've been talking about, so expect some sick jam sessions in my 'rents cellar soon. **❞**

jazzed (adjective | /dʒæzd/):

Elated, filled with energy. It's the perfect way to describe your dog every time you come home from work and he realizes that you haven't abandoned him.

Origin: A 1919 reconfiguring of the energetic music genre of the same name.

❝ I'm so jazzed for your party. Can't you tell by the jazz hands I throw up every time you mention it? ❞

jiffy (noun | /ˈdʒɪfi/):

A short period of time, like, say the amount of time it might take to eat an entire jar of Jiffy peanut butter.

Origin: *Jiffy* has been around since the 1780s, where it was used as a synonym for lightning by British thieves.

❝ Grab the jewels and get out in a jiffy! ❞

EVERYONE'S FAVORITE!

"HURRY!"
ALL PURPOSE BAKING MIX

BAKES SO FAST... GUARANTEED DRYNESS!

jive (verb / noun | /dʒaɪv/):

A word with many meanings, including "to deceive," "foolish slang talk," or "type of dance that is performed to jazz music."

Origin: Cab Calloway is one of the most well-known jazz performers of all time and was famous for his energy, fashion, and, in this case, dance moves. He popularized the jive, an energetic form of swing dancing similar to the jitterbug that was frequently performed at cakewalks and late-night music clubs. The badmouthing definitions of this word were said to have come from the dance's loud vibe.

JOMO (noun | /dʒoʊˈmoʊ/):

You've heard of FOMO, "fear of missing out" (if you haven't, feel free to flip back to the F section of this book for the entry), but have you heard of its more optimistic sister, JOMO, the joy of missing out? Unlike FOMO, which refers to negative feelings brought on by seeing other people hang out without you, JOMO represents the positive feelings associated with not having to socialize. For reference, it's the sense of relief that sweeps over you the second your drink plans cancel and you realize you have the night back to yourself.

Origin: First came FOMO. Then came JOMO. Then came a human curled up in bed with a glass of wine because no one invited her to their Halloween party and, honestly, she's not upset over it.

jonesing (adjective | /dʒoʊnzɪŋ/):

Having an insatiable craving for, like "I'm jonesing for a big, hot, steamy bowl of oatmeal."

Origin: Believe it or not, this has nothing to do with "keeping up with the Joneses." The etymology of this adjective is much more nefarious and has to do with the drug scene of the 1960s, when users would zone out (or "jones out") in the middle of the street until their high ended and they started craving ("jonesing") for another hit. How exactly the word *jones* came into the picture, though, is unclear—some connect it to male genitalia (perhaps there was a charming man named Jones who was irresistible), while others connect it to a popular street where drug dealers hung out in New York City: Jones Street.

kill (verb | /kɪl/):

To do something very well. For example, you might say to a dancer "You killed that performance!" or to a murderer "You killed that human!"

Origin: *Killing* is one of the darkest words in the English language. It's interesting, then, that it also has a large number of positive connotations, especially in the comedy world where "killing it" has referred to "making the audience helpless with laughter" since 1856. This idea of dominating a stage or a group of people eventually expanded to mean "dominating a particular area or skill," leading to this modern-day meaning.

> 66 Knock 'em dead, Albert. Seriously, break a leg. No, really, you're gonna kill it. Slay them all. 99

kween (noun | /kwin/):

A female role model. Think Ruth Bader Ginsburg, Gloria Steinem, or your roommate who parties until 4:00 a.m. and still manages to wake up on time for work the next day.

Origin: The LGBTQ community has contributed almost as many words to the English language as Shakespeare has, and that's saying something. One such contribution is "yas queen," a phrase often shouted at drag queens in the 1980s as a sign of support and encouragement. The phrase gained new momentum (and a new spelling: *kween*) in the 2010s, as internet videos and influencers revived it for the new generation.

legend (noun | /ˈlɛdʒənd/):

A person someone looks up to, like Taylor Swift, Jon Stewart, or the woman who rolls up to your local coffee shop in pajamas every morning.

Origin: The word *legend* comes from the French *légende* for "story" or "narrative." Though legendary people have been around for centuries, calling someone a legend as a term of endearment is a practice that has only really been around for a few years. TV junkies may point to *How I Met Your Mother* as the origin point for this word ("Legen—wait for it—dary!"), but that's still pending confirmation.

THE MAN *the myth* THE LEGEND A MEMOIR WITH FOREWARD BY TYLER VENDETTI

> **❝** Did you hear about that girl who got promoted straight from assistant to CEO? What a legend. **❞**

legit (adjective | /ləˈdʒɪt/):

Authentic, trustworthy, legitimate, or simply cool. Everything you'd want in a partner and/or priest. Also, an abbreviation for *legitimate* for those without the patience to say the whole word.

Origin: The word first made its debut in an 1897 review of James Corbett's recent play performance. The boxing champion had recently transitioned into the acting world (the John Cena of his day), and Hollywood types had started to question if he was "a legit." Nowadays, it's used as a shorthand for "cool" or "down-to-earth", as in "You're not a cop, right? You're legit?"

lewk (noun | /lʊk/):

A carefully constructed outfit or a very intentional choice, one that may not be entirely normal. For example, wearing pink sweatpants to a wedding is a "lewk" while wearing pink sweatpants to a funeral is "offensive."

Origin: Urban Dictionary marks the first mention of this word in 2010, but its popularity quickly grew over the course of the decade, especially as misspelling words for fun (*smol*, *kween*, etc.) took off.

66 Leopard-print pants and a polka-dotted vest? Well, that's a lewk. 99

ligma (noun | /lɪgmə/):

A made-up disease jokingly used as an excuse for not doing something. If, for example, you're too tired to go into work, but you don't have a legitimate excuse to not show up, you can claim that you have "ligma" and your boss would be none the wiser.

Origin: In May 2018, Instagrammer @ninja_hater started a rumor that video-game streamer Richard Tyler Blevins ("Ninja") had died from a bad case of "ligma." To make matters worse, Blevins had been on a flight when the rumor began, which prevented him from debunking the hoax. Luckily, the Fortnite user had a good sense of humor about the situation, eventually joining in on the joke with comments of his own like "RIP Ninja . . . that damn ligma." Since then, the word has become a catchall for any fake sickness that someone might use to get out of a situation.

lit (adjective | /lɪt/):

Exciting; intoxicated; exciting as a result of being intoxicated.

Origin: To the dismay of your seventeen-year-old, *lit* was not invented by modern-day millennials. The party word appeared much earlier than this millennium, dating back to the 1900s when people would use it to describe alcohol and drugs that "lit them up with happiness." The hip-hop community recently adopted this word, using it to describe places or events filled with "lit" people, like clubs, house parties, or the creek down the road with the firefly infestation.

❝Let's make like a lightning bug and get lit, fam.❞

lolz (noun | /lɑlz/):

Laughter. Originally an acronym for "Laugh Out Loud," *LOL* was used so frequently that it eventually became a standalone term, developing its own annoying plural *LOLZ* (as in LOLOLOLOLOLOL—or multiple *LOLs*).

Origin: Sometimes stylized as *lulz*, *lul*, or (shudder) *lollerskates*, *lolz* (or, in its singular form, *lol*) was supposedly coined by Canadian college student Wayne Pearson, who claims he and a few friends first used the expression on a private chat room in the '80s. However, others, like lexicographer Ben Zimmer, believe the term didn't come into use until later—he suggests that a 1989 technology newsletter called FidoNews was actually the first to mention the acronym. Dig deeper, though, and you'll learn that *LOL* has been around for much longer, but in a different form: it's been frequently used in letter writing as an abbreviation for "lots of love." Yes, your mom was using it right all along.

looker (noun | /ˈlʊkər/):

If you had to choose one person that you had to look at for the rest of your life, who would it be? Kevin Costner? Hayden Christensen? The guy that you had an affair with in the '80s that you haven't told a soul about? Whoever it is, they're probably a *looker*: a physically attractive person.

Origin: Apparently, the original form of this word was *good-looker* and appeared in the 1860s to describe both women and horses, which tells you everything you need to know about what kind of people used this phrase. Later, in the 1920s, looker reentered the public vocabulary, thanks in small part to the popular magazine *The Looker* and, of course, sexually charged men.

---

lowdown (noun | /ˈloʊˌdaʊn/):

All of the relevant facts or information. What you demand from your best friend after a promising date, usually through a series of texts reading "GIRL, SPILL!"

Origin: *Lowdown* was originally an adverb literally meaning "close to the ground." It later took on new meanings as an adjective for people "low" on the social ladder, specifically poor white Americans from the South or just any person one might consider "despicable." (Those are the *Oxford English Dictionary*'s words, not mine.) How it came to represent "the deets" is unclear, though it's important to point out that it did *not* come from *down-low*, a similarly structured term for "secretive."

low-key (adverb | /ˌloʊˈki/):

An adverb loosely meaning "seriously" (and sometimes "minimally") and usually said with an air of secrecy, like "Don't tell anyone but I low-key love Bratz dolls."

Origin: See: *high-key*.

lurker (noun | /ˈlərkər/):

Have you ever gone to a club with your girlfriends and noticed a brooding fellow in the corner of the room, cradling a drink while he wordlessly watches you, hoping that his distant admiration will be more flattering than creepy and you'll walk up and ask him out? That's a lurker in a modern sense of the word: someone who enters a room and quietly "lurks" in an attempt to look inconspicuous when, in reality, they end up looking more like a serial killer plotting their next move. In the digital space, the word refers to someone who enters a message board and reads all of the correspondence but doesn't participate.

Origin: With the dot-com boom came the rise of online spaces like chat rooms where people could digitally gather to discuss current events, dating, family drama, or whatever pressing issue they felt needed to be ejected into the internet void. The public nature of these spaces naturally resulted in an influx of *lurkers*: strangers who would sign onto these boards with usernames like AnonymousCat44939 and just . . . watch, reading every post but never replying themselves, like a predatory ghost.

malarkey (noun | /məˈlɑrki/):

Trivial nonsense; a word you scream at young people when their progressive opinions are clashing with your antiquated beliefs and getting on your nerves.

Origin: Though it sprang up in the 1920s, no one really knows exactly where it came from. Some suggest it derives from the Irish name Mullarkey while others think it originated with the Greek word μαλακός, meaning "soft."

mallrat (noun | /mɔlræt/):

Someone who frequently spends time at a mall, browsing the aisles of Spencer's or Pottery Barn or whatever store offers jeans for a price a teenager can afford on a Dunkin' Donuts salary.

Origin: In 1954, Victor Gruen opened the first shopping mall in Southfield, Michigan, catering to new car owners who could now drive beyond the busy, urban centers to fulfill their shopping needs. Take expanded access to suburban areas and pair it with the rise of consumerism and aging boomers on the brink of puberty, and you get a surging mall culture fueled by bored teenagers looking for a place to gather after school with their friends. The popularity of these places reached their peak in the 1980s, which is also, unsurprisingly, when this word popped up to describe the new inhabitants of these flashy megastores.

" I hate going to the mall on weekdays. It's packed with prepubescent mallrats looking for an escape from their parents. "

mom (noun | /mam/):

We're not talking about regular moms (or cool moms, for that matter) but the mom-like figure at the head of the friend group who leaps into caretaker mode the second someone has too much to drink and needs help talking through a breakup or vomiting into the toilet after too many Cosmopolitans. Every squad has a "mom" that begrudgingly nurses their friends back to good health because they just can't help themselves, and we are eternally grateful for their patience and refusal to leave us on the side of the road.

Origin: It's hard to trace the origin of this slang word simply due to the prevalence of the word *mom* in history, but it likely appeared in the late 2000s, when the word took on a new meaning as "a female figure who one looks up to or admires." The first appearance of *mom* in the context of "mom friend" specifically was in 2014, and soon ballooned into Buzzfeed's favorite subject.

❝Does your purse look like Barney's bottomless magic bag? Do you demand that your friends check in to let you know that they got home safely? Is your Facebook wall riddled with DIY crafts? If you answered yes to all of these, you might be the mom of your friend group.❞

mood (noun | /mud/):

Mood in the slang sense has nothing to do with your state of mind; rather, it describes an image, video, or piece of relatable text that inspires a certain feeling. Like when a college student rolls into an 8:00 a.m. class carrying two barrel-sized coffees—that's a mood.

Origin: Over the course of the 2010s, a number of phrases cropped up to accompany memes like TFW ("that feeling when . . ."). *Mood* joined that bandwagon in 2017, appearing on Twitter and other social media sites as a response to funny or impressive pictures or stories. It's a simple, low-effort reply that can be used for pretty much anything. A GIF of Hermione punching Malfoy in the face? Mood. A cat lazily lounging under a sunbeam? Mood. Taylor Swift making corporations kneel before her with a snap of her fingers? Big mood.

moon (verb | /mun/):

In the 1st century AD, a Roman soldier dropped his pants and bared his butt to a group of Jewish onlookers, inciting a riot that killed over thirty thousand people. Unfazed by the widespread death and titillated by the thought of making people uncomfortable, boys have continued to do this lewd activity, also known as *mooning*, for proving that yes, they really are that stupid.

Origin: The word *moon* has been a nickname for buttocks since the eighteenth century, but it didn't take on its verb meaning until the 1960s, when college students adopted the gesture as a way to distract themselves from the raging wars and dreadfully boring finals.

narc (noun | /nark/):

A tattletale; someone you can't trust with a secret, like the one about who broke the lamp in the kitchen (it was you, not the cat, we all know).

Origin: First appearing in the mid-1960s, *narc* with a *c* (like Marc with a *c*) is an abbreviated form of narcotics or, more specifically, *narcotics officer*, whose job it was to bust drug rings (hence the "snitch" definition). However, *nark* with a *k*—a British word for "police informer"—has been around for much longer, suggesting a link between the two. If that's the case, then tattling narcs/narks have been around since the nineteenth century, inspired by the Romany word *nok* meaning "nose" (which has been used as slang for "police informer" since the 1780s).

> **Don't tell anyone how complicated the etymology for narc is . . . or else, you'll be a narc.**

narrative (noun | /ˈnɛrədɪv/):

News, drama, or an activity or discussion that you'd rather not be a part of; a response that comes in handy when your mother asks you to complete a dreadfully boring task. Let me demonstrate. "Dishes? Mom, I'd like to be excluded from that narrative."

Origin: Like most great things in life, this nifty jargon came from Taylor Swift. Back in 2016, Kanye West released a song called "Famous" in which he said some unsavory things about the pop star. Tay-tay then released a statement through her publicist saying that she did not approve of Kanye's lyrics . . . to which Kanye responded by releasing a Snapchat conversation he had with her where she explicitly approves the phrase in question. When asked about this report, Swift lashed back, saying: "I would like to be excluded from this narrative, one that I have never been asked to be a part of." Though Swift has come a long way since that clip, many still use the phrase "I would like to be excluded from this narrative" as a humorous response to any uncomfortable or unwanted situation.

❝ Amy, I'm breaking up with you, but to be clear, I'd like to be excluded from this narrative, and I'd prefer that you delete my number and never speak to me again. ❞

neato (adjective | /ˈnidoʊ/):

An upbeat adjective for "cool" or, as your grandma puts it, "neat"!

Origin: First used by author Stephen Longstreet in 1951 in one of his many books. Later used by 1960s beatniks to describe unconventional social behaviors that they approved of. Eventually used by your overly supportive Aunt Jan, who thinks your decision to drop out of school and become a professional birdspotter is "totally neato!"

neck (verb | /nɛk/):

To kiss someone, sometimes on the neck, sometimes in public where bitter recently divorced onlookers can cast side glances at you and seethe at your disgusting love.

Origin: The English took the noun *neck* and made it a verb back in 1825. Though it eventually traveled overseas to the United States, another creepier term caught Americans' attention during the 1920s, overshadowing this one: *petting*. Yes, it was inspired by petting house animals and no, there's no evidence of human/animal make-outs during this time (that we could find).

> **❝** Hey, girl. Do you want to come over and neck later? Maybe we can hug too. I mean, if you want. No pressure. **❞**

nifty (adjective | /ˈnɪfti/):

Cool! Fun! Stylish! Attractive! Twee! Sweet! A word so cutesy that it must always be said in excitement!

Origin: Attributed to poet Bret Harte, who claims it is a shortened form of *magnificat*, which could either refer to Mary's Hymn of Praise for Our Lord or a cat magician, depending on your level of creativity.

> **❝** Well, this is a nifty little trinket. What did you say it was called? A machine gun? **❞**

noob (noun | /nub/):

An amateur. Someone you wouldn't entrust an important task to. Like, you wouldn't want a noob for a babysitter, or a doctor, or a hot-air-balloon pilot.

Origin: Short for *newbie* or *newb*, noob (stylized as n00b) is an internet term used to describe inexperienced computer users, specifically inexperienced gamers. This jargon stemmed from leetspeak—a digital language employed by geeks in the 1980s that involves swapping letters for numbers (hence the zeroes in n00b). When these internet aficionados stepped into the blossoming computer game culture of the 1990s, their language came with them, leading *noob* to become a term for novice players (or rather, "easy targets") in first-person shooter games—you can spot these noobs because they're the ones shooting at their own players by accident and running into walls.

> **❝** Dave, did you accidentally throw your grenade at yourself again? You're such a noob. **❞**

normcore (noun | /nɔ(ə)rmkɔ(ə)r/):

A unisex style characterized by average or normal clothes. Also extends to the attitude represented by these clothes, namely, a lack of desire to stand out from the crowd. Normcore clothing includes solid colored T-shirts or button-downs, jeans, and sneakers—really anything that a criminal might wear to blend in with the other regular, totally innocent humans.

Origin: A blend of *normal* and *hardcore*, *normcore* first appeared in the comic strip *Templar, Arizona* in 2009 or so. In it, one character is trying to explain to another all of the different subgroups that have sprung up, including the scariest one of all—normcore: "See the slight forward tilt of his chin, and the casual 'hey' with the silent H? That means he's normcore. Dangerously regular. Dresses only in T-shirts an' jeans, uses slang appropriated from other sub cultures, but only three years after its first use, an' only after it's been used in a sitcom." Years later, the cartoonist Ryan Estrada humorously acknowledged his neologism in a post titled "I'm sorry, I accidentally invented Normcore."

> **"** A Longchamp bag? An avocado enamel pin? A Coldplay CD? Mia, you've gone full normcore. **"**

numbnuts (noun | /nəmnəts/):

A dunce; an ineffectual person; someone you wouldn't choose for your kickball team (or really any team).

Origin: A similar insult, *numb head*, has been around for centuries but *numbnuts* has only been around since the 1970s, when people started purposefully conflating impotency (with *numb nuts* reflecting failing male genitalia) with stupidity.

OG (noun | /oʊdʒi/):

Someone who is authentic; an expert in one particular area; a trendsetter, like the first girl in high school to wear scrunchies.

Origin: An acronym for "original gangster," "OG" was ripped straight from the name of a real gang, the LA Gangster Crips, who rose to fame during the 1970s. It was meant to indicate that the gang was the first on the scene, and every gang that came after them were posers. It eventually adopted a reverential connotation as younger members of the gang began to use it to refer to the older, more experienced gang members. The word leaked into the rap music scene before going mainstream.

omigod (noun | /ˌoʊmaɪˈɡɑd/):

A phrase expressing shock, excitement, or amusement chiefly used by thirteen-year-old girls on their way to a Harry Styles concert.

Origin: An altered spelling of "oh my God," *omigod* interestingly enough appeared back in the 1960s as a shorthand for the full phrase. However, it really took off in the 1990s with the rise of digital forms of communication like AIM that allowed bright teens to abbreviate any and all of their thoughts, leading to the rise of letter combos like OMG (and later, the spelled-out versions like *oh em gee*). *Omigod* became one of those variations, bringing the world full circle from its 1960s roots.

> ❝ Omigod, did you see Aaron's Insta last night? It shook me. I knew I should've gone to that party. #FOMO ❞

P (adjective | /pi/):

Short for "pretty" as in "very" as in "the alphabet is P cool."

Origin: Honestly, no idea. Likely, it sprang up along during the acronym wave of the 1990s along with OMG, LMFAO, ROFL, BFF, etc.

> **"**You look P cool right now, Dee. V suave.**"**

pad (noun | /pæd/):

House, residence, abode, property, turf, dwelling, living quarters, roost, "where the hat is," whatever you call that place where you can fart without judgment and eat cereal naked just because you can.

Origin: A word exchanged in the underworld during the eighteenth century, *pad* made the rounds again in the 1960s as a beatnik word for "a place where one can sleep while intoxicated."

> **"**Wanna crash at my pad tonight? It's got a Sleep Number bed and a lava lamp, if you need more convincing.**"**

peeps (noun | /pips/):

Sugar-crusted marshmallow birds that emerge around Easter, close friends, or—for the particularly lonely people—both.

Origin: *Peeps* is short for *people*, but only those that would feel comfortable talking to you after you used this word. According to Cassell's *Dictionary of Slang* (the Bible for lingo nerds), *peeps* was popularized by college kids on 1980s campuses, though the *Oxford English Dictionary* suggests it appeared even earlier, back in the 1950s.

> " What's crackin', peeps?
> Y'all ready to par-tay? "

photobomb (verb | /ˈfoʊdoʊˌbɑm/):

You know that feeling when you walk by a group of tourists taking a selfie and you suddenly want to lurch your face into the frame for no reason other than to make a goofy face and ruin their perfect photo? This alluring, almost magnetic action is called a photobomb, and it's as natural to us as breathing or sleeping or drawing lewd photos on your drunk friend's face after they pass out.

Origin: Appearing on both Urban Dictionary and the *Oxford English Dictionary* in 2008, it's clear this word is a baby of the late 2000s, but where exactly it originated is unclear. Most sources think that it was inspired by "Google bombing," the act of searching for two unrelated words together so that they become linked on future Google searches.

> 66 One of my most cherished pictures is the one taken on my wedding day of me, my friends, and some guy in a dinosaur costume who photobombed us and then ran away, never to be seen again. 99

phub (verb | /(p)fəb/):

To play around on your phone in the presence of other people in order to purposefully snub them, as if to say, "I'd rather start another round of Doodle Jump than listen to another one of your boring stories." A useful tool on any bad first date, insufferable family dinner, or networking event filled with mansplainers.

Origin: In 2012, an Australian dictionary and an advertising agency teamed up for one very important task: to identify a common, digital-age phenomenon and invent a word for it. The action they settled on? Phubbing: purposefully ignoring someone in a social setting by paying attention to your phone instead of the conversation at hand. Though the term eventually made its way to the United States, it has been (fittingly) snubbed by many American dictionaries.

❝ So then I said, 'Sorry, Mr. President, I have enough friends!' Hey, are you listening? You're looking at your phone a lot. Are you phubbing me? ❞

piggyback (verb | /ˈpɪɡiˌbæk/):

To ride around on someone's back—fun for the rider, physically uncomfortable and occasionally painful for the ridee.

Origin: Why isn't it called "horseyback"? Good question. *Piggyback* dates back to the sixteenth century and started out as *pitch pack* and, later, *pick pack* (pick was a medieval variation of *pitch*, which was used to describe travelers pitching or throwing packs on their backs for carrying). This idea of lugging packs on one's back led to the swapping of the two terms, creating the fun term *pick-a-back*. By the nineteenth century, everyone had forgotten what *pick* meant in this context, and, I can only assume, chose a similar-sounding word that they believed made more sense—*pig*—which led to *piggyback*.

" Dad, can you give me a piggyback to the town pool? It's only five miles away; you can make it! **"**

plank (verb | /plæŋk/):

To lie flat on the ground, face down, anywhere you want, for an indefinite period of time for absolutely no discernible reason. You know what they say: kids do the darndest things . . .

Origin: Outside of the gym (where this term refers to the act of holding your body up in a pre–push up position), *planking* describes an international fad that was started by Sam Weckert, Darcy McCann, and Kym Berry of Australia; the three friends created a Facebook page where they would post pictures of each other completing this admittedly weird trend all over the country. Soon, the photos spread to the larger internet, sparking a viral meme of the same name that dominated the web throughout 2008.

plastic (adjective | /ˈplæstɪk/):

Fake or inauthentic, like the Gucci purse your mom bought on a street corner in New York. And like that purse, plastic people are stylish on the outside but empty on the inside.

Origin: While this snarky term probably made its way through high schools long before the 2000s (in the Barbie Doll sense), it didn't truly take off until the debut of *Mean Girls* in 2004, where it was used to describe the group of popular girls that would make Cady Heron's life miserable. They may not have made *fetch* happen, but they made *plastic* happen.

YOU'RE FAKE
YOU'RE FAKE
YOU'RE FAKE
YOU'RE FAKE
YOU'RE FAKE
YOU'RE FAKE
HAVE A NICE DAY

plug (verb / noun | /pləg/):

A advertisement or endorsement for one's personal agenda. You can, for example, plug your quirky words books in another one of your quirky word books, no problem! Let me show you: *The Illustrated Compendium of Ugly English Words* and *The Illustrated Compendium of Weirdly Specific Words* are both on sale now at your local bookstore. Really! Go check it out!

Origin: *Plugging* has been a part of the advertising world for a long time. Like, a *really* long time. The *Oxford English Dictionary* finds the first mention of it to be in 1902 in the sense of "to work energetically at." Nowadays, it's used in conjunction with the term *shameless* ("shameless plug") to denote a sense of pride over said advertisement, a combination that likely surfaced during the 2000s. ("Shameless plug" appeared on Urban Dictionary in 2004.)

> ❝A toast, to my best friend on her wedding day! If anyone else is looking to get married, I'm offering 50 percent off bouquet arrangements for the remainder of this ceremony. Please excuse my shameless plug! Love you, Julie!❞

poppin' (adjective | /ˈpɑpɪn/):

Exciting; awesome; popular. The sister of another equally annoying youth word: *lit*.

Origin: During the 1940s, African Americans used this term frequently to describe "lavish or reckless spending." This meaning stood the test of time, weaving its way into the hip-hop culture of the 2000s as a verb (i.e., poppin' bottles, poppin' pills, etc.). It wasn't until 2007, when Chris Brown, Lil Mama, and T.I. all released music with the word *poppin'* in the lyrics, that it reentered the mainstream.

❝ These jalapeño poppers be *poppin'*! ❞

poser (noun | /ˈpoʊzər/):

Someone who "fakes" a certain personality in order to fit in with a group or trend. The kind of people who say they like indie rock to seem hip, when they'd really rather put on Taylor Swift.

Origin: In French, *poser* means "to place" and *poseur* means "someone who places." At least, it did, until the nineteenth century when *poseur* took on a new meaning: "someone with an affected air." It entered the English language under this definition—"someone who practices the affected attitudes," which eventually extended to the modern definition—"someone who is superficial." When the 1980s rolled around and authenticity became a cherished value in American culture, the word took on a new popularity, one that stretched into the age of social media and specially curated digital profiles.

preggers (adjective | /ˈprɛgərz/):

A cute way of saying "there's a creature forming in your uterus, milking your body for nutrients and growing larger by the second, waiting for the right moment to rear its ugly head and disrupt your sleep schedule indefinitely."

Origin: Short for *pregnant*, *preggers* is actually a British term that appeared in 1942 in a novel by Monica Dickens, in which a character exclaims, "Let anyone mention in her hearing that they felt sick, and it would be all over the hospital that they were 'preggers.'" Modern television shows still exploit this fear, using sudden vomiting as a signal that the female character in question is pregnant and and that her life is about to change forever.

> ❝ Use protection, kids, or else you'll get preggers and have to drop out of school to take care of some baby named Tymothee or Hashtag or something. ❞

primo (adjective | /ˈprimoʊ/):

Prime. No, not like the Transformer. No, not like Amazon either. Like "cool" or "high quality." You know what—never mind.

Origin: From Italian *primo* meaning "first," which naturally led to similar definitions of "best" and "excellent."

> 66 That last wave was primo, bro. Knocked me sideways, but I went along for the ride. 99

props (noun | /praps/):

A compliment on a job well done. Like: "Hey, Dad, props on not saying anything embarrassing in front of my crush last week. Proud of you."

Origin: First quoted in a 1990 edition of the *Chicago Tribune*, *props* became a slang word for "due respect" that was quickly picked up by the hip-hop generation. Rappers throughout the 1990s and 2000s began to use it as a compliment to fellow rappers or cohorts whom they trusted or admired.

> 66 This pie is delicious, Ma. Props on actually making something edible. 99

psych (noun | /saɪk/):

Used to indicate the reversal of a previous statement, as in "just kidding." Commonly used in conjunction with a sassy hand motion waved in the offending person's face.

Origin: Believed to be an abbreviated version of *psychology* or *psychological*, as if the victim of the psych has been tricked psychologically. *Psych* first appeared on paper in the "just kidding" sense in Robert Chapman's *New Dictionary of American Slang* in 1986, after which point it entered high schools across the country, where students would shout it into the faces of their gullible classmates.

> ❝I love you, babe. PSYCH! I want
> to start seeing other people.❞

psyched (adjective | /saɪkt/):

Excited or otherwise characterized by intense emotion.

Origin: Pulled from the word *psychological*, as with the word *psych* above. However, this form appeared much earlier, showing up around the 1960s as a way to describe anything from crazy waves to crazy drugs.

> ❝I'm so psyched to go to sleep later.❞

psychedelic (adjective | /ˌsaɪkəˈdɛlɪk/):

Groovy. Or, for the adults, "mind-altering."

Origin: By the end of the 1950s, hallucinogenic drugs abounded in the United States, so much so that one psychiatrist named Humphry Osmond set out to invent a name for it. He sought out his friend Aldous Huxley, the soon-to-be famous author of *Brave New World*, for a suggestion. His idea? The word *phanerothyme*, from the Greek terms φανερός ("manifest") and θύμος ("spirit"). Osmond liked the sound of it, but gave it a slight twist, turning it into *psychedelic* and changing the way we talked about these loopy drugs for the rest of time. Eventually, the name of the drugs, "psychedelics," and the feeling the drugs produced came to mean one and the same, leading to this adjective.

❝ Have you ever watched fireworks through a kaleidoscope? It's positively psychedelic, man. ❞

punk (noun | /pəŋk/):

A brat or a troublemaker, the kind your mom has banned from sleepovers.

Origin: What began as an adjective that meant "bad" or "inferior" in the late 1800s turned into "a bad guy" when its other common slang definition—a homosexual man—blended with this one. The connection was cemented in the late '70s with the rise of the punk rock genre, which attracted eccentric or troublesome boys who wanted to stick it to the man.

pwn (verb | /poʊn/):

To destroy someone in an online game, with no regards for their feelings or their self-respect. Yes, Dad, I'm talking to you. I pwned you in Minesweeper one time, you need to get over it.

Origin: According to a number of very serious and well-researched reports, *pwn* originated from a typo. Yup. Sometimes the simplest answer is the right one.

❝ Please don't pwn me, bro. Online solitaire is my only hobby. It's all I have. Don't take this away from me. ❞

QT (noun | /ˈkjuˈti/):

A cutie. Sometimes written as QT 3.14, for all you nerds looking for a pick-up line.

Origin: Most likely another by-product of texting's original character limit that forced most teenagers to communicate through messages resembling alphabet soup.

> **66** Luv u no mtr wat, QT. 4evr n evr. **99**

quality (adjective / noun | /ˈkwɔlədi/):

An item or a person that is top-notch. A boyfriend can be quality. A diamond ring can be quality. A ten-year-old lambic beer that costs ten thousand dollars for a sip can be quality. It's all about perspective.

Origin: Hard to tell when this adjective became a member of the jargon club. Obviously, the word has been around for centuries, but its entry into the slang world is a little less clear: it first appeared in Urban Dictionary in 2003, so that's probably the best bet.

> **66** These Wild Berry Skittles are *quality*, with a capital Q. **99**

radical (adjective | /ˈrædək(ə)l/):

Beyond cool. Like, so cool that that the word cool doesn't even cut it anymore, so you have to resort to words that your parents once used.

Origin: *Radical* comes from the Latin word *radicalis* meaning "root." This makes sense when you look at *radical*'s political connections, all of which take place at the root of the problem. For example, many politicians use the term *radical* as a cry for major change (i.e., radical reformation). In the 1970s, surfers adopted the term as a way to describe things that they cannot change and are at the limits of their control (i.e., waves, if I had to guess).

rags (noun | /rægz/):

Dirty clothes; the name of your childhood dog.

Origin: A word as old as time; it has been around since the 1300s and was likely invented by a posh older woman who saw a less fortunate person wearing old, dirty-looking clothes and equated them to dishrags. This is not backed by any sources, but I'd put my money on it.

66 Get out of those rags and into something presentable. We're going to Easter dinner, not a peasants' ball. 99

rando (noun | /ˈrændoʊ/):

A stranger; someone you definitely shouldn't talk to, especially if they're offering you candy.

ratchet (adjective | /ˈrætʃət/):

Put simply, a hot mess. Picture what you look like when you roll out of bed every morning. Now double that. Now stick that through a hornet's nest, then a washing machine. What you have left is ratchet.

Origin: Another contribution from the hip-hop community, *ratchet* appeared as early as 1998, showing up in a song from E-40 called "Lieutenant Roast a Botch." Though it originally referred to a crazed Southern woman (the word itself likely formed from the butchering of "wretched"), the African American community reclaimed the word at the turn of the century, molding it into an endearing term and weaving it into popular culture. Beyoncé was even seen wearing a pair of earrings reading "ratchet" in 2012, so we're all officially allowed to like it.

> **❝** I walked through a dust storm on my way to school today, so I'm sorry if I look a little ratchet. **❞**

read _{(noun | /rɛd/):}

Let's set the scene: it's 1:00 a.m., raining, and you're about to confess your love to your two-month-long crush via text. Fingers shaking, perspiration building, you press "Send." And you wait. And you watch. And you see a four-letter word appear below your text: "Read." And then? Silence. Your heart sinks, your mind races, and, for a second, you consider shoving your phone in a garbage disposal, fleeing the country, and adopting a new identity (you could be a Cheryl, you think, or a Patti)—all to avoid having to show up to school the next day and face the boy that received your text and left you on "Read."

Origin: We can thank Steve Jobs for this nerve-racking noun. Days after he died in October 2011, his company, Apple, announced a new app that would revolutionize digital communication: iMessage. This feature allowed real-time texting for any two people who were connected to WiFi, which is to say, you could, for the first time, see your friend "bubbling" when they were typing out a text to you. Another thing it could do? Send read receipts—little messages below every text indicating whether the person on the other end of the phone had read your text. This simple feature, intended to foster transparency, instead sparked anxiety in iPhone users everywhere, who were now forced to wonder why so-and-so had seen their text and ignored it. This sense of insecurity became linked to the word *read* itself, turning it into a general slang word for "the state of being seen but ignored."

> **"** Bart, this is your girlfriend. Are we hanging out this weekend or not? I have sent you seven texts today, and you've ignored every one. If you keep leaving me on read, you're not going to have a girlfriend come Monday. **"**

realness (noun | /ˈri(ə)lnəs/):

The ability to emulate authenticity, whether that's by sticking your neck out selflessly for a friend or happily giving every single person in class a Valentine.

Origin: First a serious word for "an object that exists," *realness* joined the realms of slang in the 1980s, when drag balls emerged in NYC as a safe space for LGBTQ men to express themselves. At these events, men would group together into "houses" and perform various tasks in order to win exclusive titles like Femme Queen. One category that was sometimes invoked was "realness": the ability to pass as a heterosexual. Though many artists have attempted to shed light on ball culture (Madonna's video for "Vogue" actually borrowed moves from this period in hopes of spreading awareness), none have done it better than RuPaul, whose widely popular *Drag Race* series has reinvigorated this once taboo activity. In doing so, he's allowed words like *realness* to be reclaimed by the queer community; rather than represent one's success in "faking it," the word has flipped to represent authenticity.

❛❛ Brad, everyone sees you as the dumb, blond quarterback. Joining the spoken-word team is really going to bring out your realness. **❜❜**

receipts (noun | /riˈsits/):

Physical evidence in the form of screenshots, social media posts, text histories, etc., that proves or disproves a claim. Can be employed on a small scale (when you want to prove that your friend did, in fact, say the thing she's claiming she never said) or a large scale (when you want to prove that the president of the United States did the bad thing that he's been denying).

Origin: There was no one person who invented receipts; it's a gift to the English language that we can all claim for ourselves. That's because *receipts* as a word for "physical paper displaying proof of purchase" has existed for years, so it's hard to tell exactly when its slang counterpart appeared. One source points to a 2002 interview with Whitney Houston in which she denies buying a large amount of drugs, yelling "I wanna see the receipts." From here, it's believed that the phrase "show me the receipts" and eventually just "receipts" formed and slinked its way into local politics and celebrity gossip magazines.

> **"** Oh, don't try to pretend like you didn't like the Brony documentary, Tina. I have the receipts. **"**

rekt (adjective | /rɛkt/):

Imagine someone asking, "What if we take the word *wrecked*, but make it edgier?" That's *rekt*. This adjective is defined as "destroyed, but in a playful way." It's the kind of comment you'd make to a friend as he walks into the bar on his twenty-first birthday, as in "Get rekt, James, before you have a wife and kids and a mortgage and regrets!"

Origin: Functioning both as a form of smack talk and a form of encouragement, *rekt* began in the United States as a jocular jab used by gamers before entering a competition, like the phrase "bring it on." In the United Kingdom, though, it had another meaning—to get wasted—which has led to this word having two definitions: "losing badly in a game or contest" or simply "drunk."

❝ It's a Friday and I've got three bottles of wine in my fridge. Time to get rekt. ❞

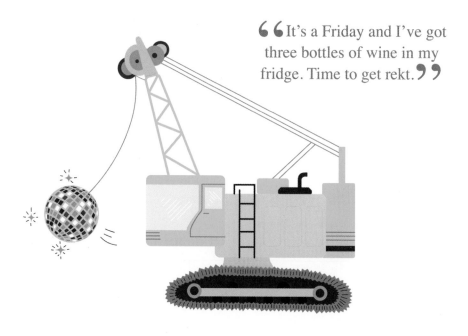

respek (noun | /rəˈspɛk/):

R-E-S-P-E-C-T. Ask Aretha, she knows.

Origin: When a rapper named Birdman was mocked on a radio show over his title, he clapped back with "Put some respek on my name!"—a line that went so viral, he ended up launching a whole line of merchandise with the word branded across the front.

> ❝I'm your mother's friend's sister's boyfriend's father! Show me some respek!❞

righteous (adjective | /ˈraɪtʃəs/):

Amazing. Usually said by a guy wearing sunglasses and a poncho.

Origin: Back in the day (Jesus's day, that is) *righteous* meant "morally upright," which, I think we can all agree, is good. In fact, that's how the two meanings converged: many believed that righteous people were excellent, leading *righteous* to literally mean "excellent." As time went on, this adjective got passed around from generation to generation, starting with the hepcats of the jazz age, then moving onto the hipsters, and finally ending with the surfer bros of the 1980s.

> ❝That wave was downright *righteous*. I think it literally knocked the sin straight out of me.❞

riot (noun | /ˈraɪət/):

A hilarious person or situation. Your father is a riot. Your barista is a riot. Your coworker who puts on sunglasses when the office lights are too bright is a riot. She's also a little dramatic, but you already knew that.

Origin: Though *riot* as a noun for "violent gathering" comes from the Old French *riote* meaning "quarrel," the slang version was likely pulled from theater lingo of the early 1900s—an act was said to be a riot if the audience offered thundering applause and demanded an encore (perhaps threateningly, which would explain the connection to the original definition).

❝ Wow, Mom, the way you made that bellhop cry for dropping all of our luggage in the pool? That was a *riot*. ❞

ripped (adjective | /rɪpt/):

Muscular. Not in a "I go to the gym sometimes" way but more of a "I walked into the gym and had the owner begging me to be the face of the company within five seconds" way.

Origin: Bodybuilding was all the rage in the 1970s and '80s, giving birth to its own set of vocab words like *spotter*, *jacked*, and this one: *ripped*. However, *ripped* did not originally refer to the size of one's muscles (like it often is today) but the definition of one's muscles—how sculpted or shapely they looked, and whether or not one's veins appeared to be ripping through the skin.

NEW YEAR, NEW ME!

❝Dude, have you been drinking the Muscle Milk I gave you for Christmas? Because you looked ripped!❞

salty (adjective | /ˈsɔlti/):

Bitter. Resentful. Likely to increase the blood pressure of those over the age of sixty-five. Delicious.

Origin: If you think this word is connected to the Morton Salt Company meme, you'd be right—in 2014, a meme depicting the girl in the yellow raincoat featured on Morton Salt Company products began circulating on the internet with the caption "Don't be a salty b****!"—which led the American Dialect Society to crown it as that year's "most likely to succeed" neologism. But what you might not know is that this word predates our yellow lady friend, stretching back to the 1860s when *salty* became associated with saltwater sailors who were known for their vulgarity. Some have even found evidence of the word (in the form of *salty b*****) dating back to the late 1700s as a nickname for dogs in heat.

❝ I know I hacked into your computer and stole the research on cocker spaniel genetics that ultimately won me the Nobel Prize, but you don't need to be so salty about it. ❞

scarf (verb | /skarf/):

To eat quickly. What moths do to all of the unattended scarves in your home.

Origin: It's generally believed that this slang term appeared in America around the 1960s, though no one seems to know how. The best guess is that it came from the word *scoff* ("to eat greedily"), which came from the word *scaff* (Scottish dialect for "to beg for food"), which at some point along the way gained an *r* and turned this wintertime staple into a favored verb for hangry people everywhere.

❝ I'm so starving, I could scarf down a horse and still have room for dessert. ❞

score (verb | /skɔ(ə)r/):

To successfully hook up with someone; to construct the soundtrack for a feature film; to get something you want, like a winning lottery ticket or a hug from your parents. Can also be shouted in excitement whenever one of the three aforementioned things happens.

Origin: In the sexual sense, *score* grew out of an American 1960s slang phrase "to score between the posts." I'll let you connect the dots.

❝ Wait, this piece of chocolate has caramel in it, *and* it's shaped like Laura Dern's face? SCORE! ❞

scrub (noun | /skrəb/):

Someone who is straight-up bad at something. More specifically, a guy who is bad at relationships, has no job or money, lives with his momma, thinks he's fly, and hangs out of the passenger side of his best friend's ride and tries to holler at women who are totally uninterested.

Origin: A slang word for a contemptible person (in particular, a prostitute) since the 1500s, *scrub* gained widespread attention in the 1990s with the release of TLC's hit song "No Scrubs" and their public dismissal of "broke men."

scuttlebutt (noun | /ˈskʌt(ə)lbʌt/):

Another word for "rumor" that Adele *should've* used in her hit song "Rumor Has It." (Guess we'll never know what "Scuttlebutt Has It" would've sounded like.)

Origin: Early ships were fastened with a device called a *scuttlebutt* that stored water for seamen to drink from on their long journeys. When these sailors began gathering around the scuttlebutts to swap stories, though, the word took on a new meaning and eventually came to embody the rumors themselves, making scuttlebutts the original water cooler conversations.

selfie (noun | /ˈsɛlfi/):

A photo of oneself, taken by oneself, for oneself (or for the 'gram).

Origin: Once upon a time, there was an Australian man who posted a picture of himself online with a swollen lip that he got after having one too many beverages at a mate's birthday party and tumbling face first into the concrete. Though the young man had only wanted advice on whether or not he should get stitches, what he got instead was worldwide attention for the cutesy moniker that he used to describe the photo—*selfie*—altering the course of photography as we know it.

served (verb | /sərvd/):

To get owned, a.k.a. to be publicly embarrassed by another party who has outperformed you in some way. Often said with attitude by some smug kid who was born while you were still in college.

Origin: The idea of "getting served" originates from the legal act of serving someone a document that demands a response (therefore signaling to the person that they can't get away with whatever stint they tried to pull). But I'd be remiss to not mention another, lesser known history involving pimps and a highly entertaining court case. *Served* in the criminal underworld refers to a scenario in which a pimp steals another pimp's client. This all-too-common event was forced into the spotlight in 2005 in a court case titled United States of America v. Charles Floyd Pipkins, a.k.a. Sir Charles, Andrew Moore, Jr., a.k.a. Batman, in which one pimp, Worm, got mad when another pimp, Fantastic, stole his girl. What followed was a hilariously documented legal battle which resulted in a slew of petty dialogue and a whole lot of jail time. Ask your local law professor for the details.

shade (verb / noun | /ʃeɪd/):

An insult best served cold and subtly. Can be used as a verb as in "Girl, are you a palm tree because you're throwing some major shade?" and the like.

Origin: Shade can be attributed both to Jane Austen and the gay community (what's not to love?), appearing first in Jane Austen's 1814 novel Mansfield Park and later in the ball culture of the 1980s. (For more information on that, see: *drag*.)

> 66 Don't pretend like you're not mad. I can practically feel your shade. 99

ship (verb | /ʃɪp/):

When you see a high schooler staring off into space, eyes glossed over like little glass balls and an expression so blank, you could draw doodles on it, there's only one thing they could possibly be thinking about: shipping, a.k.a. mentally placing people (like, say, the student and a hot, older teacher) in a relationship with each other.

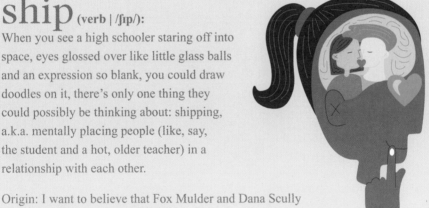

Origin: I want to believe that Fox Mulder and Dana Scully were soulmates . . . and apparently, so does everyone else. This term (short for *relationship*) saw its origin in 1995 across message boards for the widely popular TV show *The X-Files*. It was there that fans coined the word *shipping* in response to their belief that Fox and Dana should be in a relationship. That's the truth, and yes, it is pretty out there.

shook (adjective | /ʃʊk/):

Surprised to the core, like someone poured your brain into a cocktail shaker and spun it around. Plenty of things can make one feel "shook," including a shocking news story, an impressive clapback, or an HD picture of Jeff Goldblum staring straight into the camera.

Origin: The word *shook* (sometimes written as *shooketh*) has been around longer than most, dating as far back as the 1800s, when it was used to describe religious experiences that actually shook people. It then found a place among Australian, Irish, and American drinkers, who often found themselves "shook" (read: drunk) after one too many drinks. Then, in 1995, a hip-hop group named Mobb Deep dropped the word in one of their songs, "Shook One," and the music community welcomed the term with open arms, peppering it into their lyrics until the term took on a life of its own.

❝ Have you seen that photo of Chris Evans holding a kitten in his Captain America uniform? I am shook. ❞

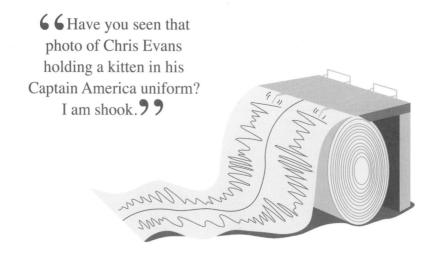

sick (adjective | /sɪk/):

So awesome that it's nearly nauseating. Like, if whatever-it-is induced vomiting, you wouldn't mind, because your life would be overall better for having seen it.

Origin: *Sick* was a staple of 1980s skateboarding culture in the United States, first appearing in print a campus slang guide for University of North Carolina, Chapel Hill, in 1983. How it ended up there, though, is a subject of debate. Many internet scholars (read: linguistic nerds and online forum users who wholeheartedly believe themselves to be academics) claim that it in fact originated in the 1980s, but in South London, where it was appropriated by black youth interested in the growing "grime" music scene (one that would eventually morph into the more widely known "dubstep" genre). Others think that it formed out of *bad*—a slang word with similar connotations that predates *sick* by a few dozen years.

❝ That scar bisecting your face into squares, making it look like a tic-tac-toe board? It's sick. ❞

sis (noun | /sɪs/):

Sister, from the same mister or another mister.

Origin: If orange is the new black, then *sis* is the new *bro* and has been since about 2016 when it first started popping up. While some may see it as a chummy word for "female friend," others point to a deeper history, one where *sis* is used by LGBTQ and African American groups as an empowering, gender-bending colloquialism that challenges heteronormative structures. Put simply, *sis* is a subtle way for queer or minority groups to dictate their own labels much in the same way as *sista* or *kween*.

sketch (adjective | /skɛtʃ/):

An unmarked ice-cream truck parked outside of a college dorm at midnight? That's sketch. A Facebook invitation to a "makeup product party" from some girl you took an improv class with two years ago and haven't spoken to since? That's sketch. A gutter clown promising to dissolve all of your student debt if you would just, please, come a little closer? That's tempting but still very sketch.

Origin: When someone says, "show me your sketch of Bob Ross," you're not expected to unveil a fully complete drawing of the famed American paint instructor. That's because a *sketch* in the traditional sense is a "light or rough drawing or outline," and it is this very sense of incompleteness that led to the contemporary meaning of this slang term—a "sketchy" situation is one that you may not have confidence in due to its fuzzy details. Though it's unclear when exactly this change happened, most records show the word *sketchy* popping up in the 1990s, right on time to describe sketchy internet websites and message-board users.

> ❝ Did you see that guy standing outside with the 'Give me your wallet for a surprise! I promise I will not steal it!' sign? Seems a bit sketch. ❞

skinny (noun | /ˈskɪni/):

The truth, the gossip, and everything in between.

Origin: We can salute the United States military for this word, which was coined by soldiers during the WWII era. How it came about, though, is still up for debate, with some saying it was inspired by the phrase "the naked truth" (picture a skinny, naked lieutenant confessing his crimes), while others think it may have come from the skinny papers that soldiers received their missives on. This is why it's often used as part of the larger phrase: "Did you get the skinny?"

> ❝ Hey, madre, what's the skinny on dinny?
> I'm hankering for some Sloppy Joe's. ❞

sksksk (noun | ˈsksksk):

Presenting . . . the new LOL. According to most traditional dictionaries, *sksksk* is not an official word, but its sheer popularity online and among "VSCO girls" (we'll get to that) makes this "light chuckle" a term worth highlighting.

Origin: In 2012, Visual Supply Company released a photo-editing app called VSCO that allowed users to fine-tune their dinner shots and selfies, creating final products that look like they were pulled straight from an advanced college photography course. These "VSCO girls," as they were called, began to develop a culture all their own comprised of Birkenstocks, painfully normcore clothes, and sksksk: a tsk-esque laugh used to express excitement, shock, or discomfort, as if the person on the other end of the computer had become overwhelmed and slid their face across the keyboard.

slaps (adjective | /slæps/):

Slaps is an interesting word in that it's difficult to define exactly what it is: an adjective, a verb, a noun, a pigeon? It's all very unclear. That's because it's usually nestled into a phrase like "That slaps!" which is youth-talk for "That song or comedian or toothbrush you just showed me was knee-slappingly good!"

Origin: Rumored to have started in the Bay Area, *slaps* (or sometimes *slappers*) could be the result of a number of things: it may have started as a mix of clapping and snapping (both signs of musical appreciation), or, alternatively, it may simply be a reference to the feeling produced when the bass drops and practically slaps the ground and the eardrums.

❝ Have you heard of that band, The Beatles? Their music really slaps. ❞

slay (verb | /sleɪ/):

Despite the images that the word *slay* might be conjuring in your brain (let me guess: vampires?), this millennial word actually refers to the much less violent act of successfully achieving something. For example, if you slay a donkey-riding competition, it means you probably have a blue first-place ribbon in your future. If you slay a donkey, you may be in for a very nasty visit from your local farmer.

Origin: There's evidence that, during the 1920s, *slay* originally meant "to make someone laugh hysterically" (similar to, say, "knock 'em dead") before it evolved into a supportive cry for drag queens in 1970s and '80s ball culture (i.e., "Slay, girl, slay!"). Building on this popularity, Beyoncé incorporated the term into her 2016 song "Formation," launching it into the mainstream.

❝ You know what they say . . . Beyoncé knows how to slay. ❞

smol (noun | /smɔl/):

Small, but in a cute way. The counterpart of *tol* ("tall").

Origin: Somewhere in the 2010s, misspellings became "cool," leading to words like *kween*, *rekt*, and this little nugget. While it had already taken over the interwebs by 2015, its exact origin is uncertain; fans of the band Twenty One Pilots claim they are responsible, citing their fondness for the nickname "smol bean" in reference to the group's lead singer Tyler Joseph, but, more likely, it sprang up as part of the aforementioned misspelling movement.

> "Hi, everyone! This is my tol, Derek, and I am his smol, Minnie. Nice to meet you!"

snacc (noun | /snæk/):

A person so attractive, you want to gobble them up, and not in a grandma kind of way.

Origin: Originally a term for male genitalia in the 1970s and '80s, *snacc* reemerged in 2009 as a term for "a tasty treat" and eventually "the human equivalent of a tasty treat."

> "My cat's so thicc from all those snaccs I'm givin' her."

snap (verb / noun | /snæp/):

Sometimes the simplest answer is the right one: *snap* refers to the social app Snapchat, in which users can exchange photos and videos that will disappear after they're viewed. If a child is demanding that you "send them a snap" or that "you snap them back so they don't lose their 473 streak," what they're really asking is that you send them a selfie as soon as possible. Doesn't even have to be good. Doesn't even have to be a selfie. Could be a two-second video of your hairy big toe. Whatever keeps the streak alive.

Origin: Snapchat came out in 2012 and this term immediately followed, dominating the list of social media slang words until Instagram messenger and Twitter took off and ushered in its replacement: *DM* (direct message).

> **❝** I sent you a snap of my wedding dress literally two seconds ago and you haven't responded! What's the deal? **❞**

snatched (adjective | /snatʃt/):

Next time you're eyeing that cutie behind the coffee counter, try calling them *snatched* instead of *on fleek*. If they're tapped into pop culture, they'll know you're trying to call them attractive. If they're not, they'll call security. It's a risk, sure, but getting out of your comfort zone is the only way to truly grow.

Origin: Hailing from the drag culture of the 1990s, *snatched* came to be when African American women sporting weaves started using it to describe something so impressive, it could actually "snatch" their hair off. With the premiere of shows like *RuPaul's Drag Race*, drag culture came back to life in a big way, bringing words like *snatched* with it.

snazzy (adjective | /ˈsnazi/):

Flashy, elegant, with just the right amount of *z*s.

Origin: First recorded in the 1930s by Americans still riding the Roaring
Twenties high who needed a new way to describe themselves that wasn't *snappy*
or *jazzy*. At a loss for other options, they settled on a hybrid of the two, creating
snazzy.

**❝Lookatchu, with
your purple dress and
your green shoes and
your giant dinosaur face.
Barney, you're looking
snazzy this evening.❞**

spaz (noun | /spæz/):

An easily excitable person, the kind that responds in all caps when you share insignificant updates like "my credit score went up two points" and "I've decided I like Anne Hathaway again."

Origin: This term has a grave history. It comes from the term *spastic*, which in the medical world describes the condition spastic paralysis—a nervous system disorder that causes the host to lose motor coordindination and, as a result, shake unpredictably. At some point in the '50s, *spaz* was adopted as a tasteless nickname for clumsy people and, later, "hyper" people who had so much energy, they appeared to be vibrating or "spasming."

> **❝Did someone slip you an espresso or something? You're acting like a spaz.❞**

split (verb | /splɪt/):

To leave abruptly and usually without telling anyone so as to avoid any conversations about "catching up sometime" or "why you're leaving the party early, you've only been here for thirty minutes, did I do something wrong, was it not *fun* enough??"

Origin: *Split* in the divorce sense popped up in the 1940s, but this less-devastating term came later, showing up in the 1950s and 1960s as a hip way to exit an event, as if you are divorcing it. (This might be a stretch, but it's the only logical explanation.).

> **❝Let's make like a banana and split.❞**

squad (noun | /skwad/):

A friend group. If famous, a squad is composed of two to six high-profile models, actresses, writers, or influencers that are willing to travel to exotic locations on a whim for an Instagram photoshoot. If non-famous, a squad is composed of two to six annoyingly supportive high school friends with regular, human jobs who have seen your ugly-cry face and still continue to talk to you.

Origin: *Squad* has a long and complicated history that predates Taylor Swift: in the early days of wartime (think the 1600s), men would arrange themselves into square formations heading into battle. Named after the Latin word for square (*quadratum*), these *squadrons* became the inspiration for the word *squad*. The sense of solidarity built into these groups lent itself to the modern definition of "friend group," which Taylor Swift capitalized on in the early 2010s by carefully constructing a pack of high-powered women and labeling them her #squad on social media, forever altering the language of female friendship.

> ❝ All right, squad. Coachella is in five days and we haven't even nailed down our buddy system pairings. Let's get it together. ❞

square (noun | /skwɛː/):

What's cooler than a square? Pretty much everything. I'm talkin' circles, triangles, pentagons, you name it. And don't even get me started on parallelograms.

Origin: *Square* derives from the French word *esquire* (recognize it?), which somehow came to mean "honest" around the 1500s (hence phrases like "fair and square"). But hundreds of years later (in the 1940s, to be exact), *square* was adopted by jazz enthusiasts as a derogatory term for tone-deaf friends who couldn't appreciate their music tastes; the nickname derives from the square formations that conductors use when directing simple, four-chord songs (as if to say, "you're so basic, you could never fully understand how great Duke Ellington is").

“ Are you coming bungee jumping with me or not? It's only a 500-foot drop; don't be a square. **”**

stan (verb / noun | /stæn/):

To support something or someone in an obsessive manner by either fanatically posting about them on Twitter or locking them in your house for weeks and pushing them to churn out new work until they're forced to smash you over the head with an antique typewriter in order to escape.

Origin: Interestingly, this term comes from the 2000 song of the same name by Eminem, who describes an overzealous fan literally named Stan. The next year, another rapper, Nas, released a song that employed Stan as a noun for the first time ever: "You a fan, a phony, a fake . . . a stan." From there, it evolved into a verb and, eventually, a major staple in digital culture.

❝We stan Stephen King.❞

steez (noun | /stiz/):

Someone's distinct style, like a personal brand but for clothes; something we all want, but can never have.

Origin: *Steez*—or style with ease—was first dropped by Method Man in a 1995 song and later in a 1998 Gang Starr track. From there, it diverged into two different paths, entering the hip-hop world as a fashion descriptor and the sports world as a word for someone's snowboarding or skiing aesthetic.

❝Banana-printed button-ups are my steez now.❞

stoked (adjective | /stoʊkd/):

Excited to do something; a feeling that all humans, I would hope, experience at some point in their life.

Origin: This seventeenth-century word was once used to describe the rekindling of a fire, and we still use it when we say, "I stoked the flames." But, by the 1960s, it had been claimed by California surfers as a term for "excited." (You know when a fire whips around in the wind like an erratic inflatable tube man? Imagine harnessing that energy and sticking it inside a sun-kissed surfer bro—that's *stoked*.)

> **"Bruh, are you stoked for our next No Shirt-No Pants-No Problem surf day or what?"**

stompers (noun | /ˈstɒmpəs/):

Shoes. Big shoes, little shoes, wide shoes, cute-but-will-definitely-give-me-a-blister shoes, all shoes.

Origin: Supposedly appeared in 1899, but beyond that not much else is known, except for the fact that shoes that leave lattices in the dirt are called wafflestompers, which is how all boots should be referred to from now on.

  ❝ Another cockroach, huh? Ah, don't you worry, I'll take the little cretin out with my stomper. ❞

streak (noun | /strik/):

If you've never used the social media app Snapchat, then you probably don't know about streaks: the state of having a consistent correspondence with another user, causing a little fire emoji to pop up next to their name with a little number sign indicating how many days that messages have been exchanged. In layman's terms, streaks are like the digital version of the don't-drop-the-ball game, where you throw a ball back and forth with another friend as many times as possible until one of you gives up or dies, resetting the streak to zero.

Origin: Referring both to the record itself and friends who help create them, *streaks* or *snapstreaks* cropped up in 2016 when the app developers first released the feature, sparking a slew of dramatic articles like "Teens explain the world of Snapchat's addictive streaks, where friendships live or die" and "Snapchat streak lost? How to file a claim and get your snapstreak back."

  ❝ What am I doing this weekend? Not much, really, probably just partying with my streaks. ❞

studmuffin (noun | /ˈstəd͵məf(ə)n/):

An attractive man, one that's as appetizing as a muffin. (Not like, a corn muffin. A chocolate-chip muffin, maybe.)

Origin: In a 1993 edition of the *The New York Times Magazine*, author William Safire explained the genesis of *studmuffin*, noting that it surfaced in response to the nickname *muffin*, which, at the time, was a condescending quip that men used to put women down. In retaliation, women coined an equally condescending term: *studmuffin* (in reference to male horses, which are studs). If a studmuffin hits the gym enough, he can level up into a diesel or, if he's especially ambitious, a Vin Diesel.

> **❝** Listen, studmuffin, I'm in the middle of running a multibillion-dollar business, so I don't have time to listen to you recap your workout routine. **❞**

suh (int. | /sʌ/):

Sup, but with a pinch of sleepiness.

Origin: It appears to have blossomed in 2018(ish) as a combination of *sup* and *huh*, creating a word that is both a greeting and an expression of curiosity.

❝ Suh, man? Wanna get some fro-yo or something? ❞

supermurgitroid

(adjective | /supər'mʊrgitrɔɪd/):

Cool; mind-blowing, like the fact that this word really existed and people used it.

Origin: The internet provided no answers and neither did the grandparents that were surveyed, so I've got nothing other than the fact that it was a slang term from the 1950s jazz era of American history.

❝ That riff was supermurgitroid, hepcat. ❞

sus (noun | /səs/):

Suspicious. Need an example? The car idling outside of your house with "free hugs" etched into the side is sus. So is the "I love you!" message penned in blood on the bathroom mirror and the lengthy voice mails of someone breathing that keep popping up on your answering machine. In fact, your entire life seems pretty sus. You might want to consider moving.

Origin: This word, it seems, originated in the United Kingdom many moons ago as a name for the rampant stop-and-frisk laws that allowed police to pull over anyone they deemed "a suspected person." Such practices continued into the 1970s and '80s, hopping across the pond over to the US, where minority groups began actively fighting against these sus laws. Eventually, *sus* was extended to "suspect" things in general.

> **"** I wanted to go out with him again but he started acting sus all of a sudden, asking me for my address and Social Security number and my mom's maiden name. **"**

swag (noun | /swæg/):

Someone who exudes confidence, either as a result of their style or the inflated ego that they were born with. Can also refer to small goods that one is gifted, like a box of tiny shampoos or pens branded with your company logo that are handed out at the annual Christmas party instead of bonuses.

Origin: The latter sense of the word started in the eighteenth century, when stolen goods were referred to as *swag* and the satchels they were stuffed into as *swag bags*. This meaning ultimately led to *swagger* and then back to the shorter form *swag* in the twenty-first century, and was used to refer to someone with loads of confidence like, say, a thief.

“To celebrate Earth Day, we're giving away free vegan swag bags! Yes, of course there's kale!”

swell (adjective | /swɛl/):

Wonderful, like the flower shop owner who makes it a point to squeeze this word into every conversation.

Origin: In a medical sense, *swell*, as we know, describes the inflammation of a wound, causing it to grow in size. This idea of an increase in size or intensity became equated to an increase in power, leading to another definition of the word: "a distinguished person." This eventually turned into "a pleasant person," then "pleasant," and, finally, "OK." Talk about a downgrade.

“You can go skiing and sunbathing in the same day? Wow, California really *is* swell.”

swerve (verb | /swərv/):

To avoid a person or a subject that one doesn't want to deal with, like your neighbor Gloria who has already stopped by three times this morning to ask why you didn't come to her Herbalife party yesterday. (Because Herbalife is a pyramid scheme, Gloria! They're playing you, can't you see that?!)

Origin: In 2012, Kanye West, Big Sean, Pusha T, and 2 Chainz collaborated on a song called "Mercy" in which they describe avoiding a gold-digging lady by "swerving"; the whole world has since swerved with them.

66 Liana just brought up buying tickets to that Geek Bowl event in the group thread again. SWERVE! 99

swing (verb | /swɪŋ/):

When someone says they're going to "swing by," they're not saying that they're going to fly in on a floating tire swing like some knockoff magic carpet. They're saying that they're going to visit soon, so you should probably throw away those empty Chinese food containers littering your living room, stat.

Origin: A 1960s Americanism, it seems to be derived from the use of automobiles to quickly swerve around unexpectedly, as if you're turning into someone's driveway without warning.

❝ Hey, Jim . . . it's funny, I don't remember you saying that you were going to swing by tonight. And yet, here you are. **❞**

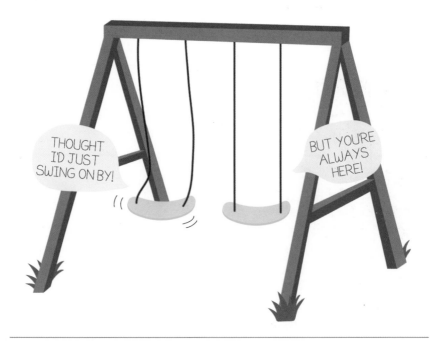

swole (noun / adjective | /ˈswəʊl/):

Ripped; a gym rat or a gym human. Really, anything muscle-y. The species is irrelevant.

Origin: *Swole* is nothing new: it's been the past tense of the verb *swell* for ages, until better-sounding conjunctions like *swollen* took over. However, its use as a bodybuilding term didn't manifest until the 1990s, appearing early on in Ice T's 1991 song "The Tower," among others, as a compliment akin to "fit." Why? It's unclear, though it seems it may be because muscular arms look swollen, like they're bulging balloons that could pop at any moment.

> 66 You're looking swole today, Dwayne. Have you been pumping iron like I told you? 99

szn (noun | /ˈsiːz(ə)n/):

Season, but abbreviated. Can refer to astrological seasons ("Gemini szn"), sports seasons ("Pats szn"), or literal seasons ("pretty leaf szn").

Origin: This one seems to have come from Kanye West who, in his 2013 song "On Sight," bragged about the upcoming "Yeezy season." For those of you who don't know, *Yeezy* is one of the rapper's many nicknames. This means the man accidentally invented a slang term by bragging about his own popularity, which may be the most Kanye thing to ever happen.

> 66 'Tis the szn. 99

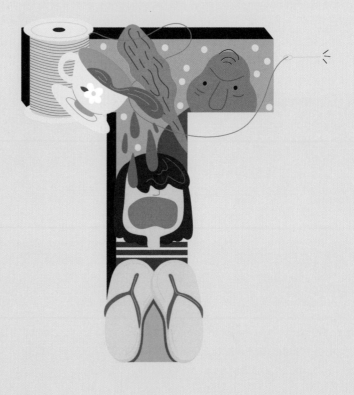

tattletale (noun | /ˈtat(ə)lteɪl/):

Someone who snitches and will probably, at some point, be getting stitches. You know how it goes.

Origin: Take the word *tell-tale* and mix it with *tattle* and you'll get this sneaky little hybrid.

> **❝**I know I shouldn't have stuffed Sean's favorite Beanie Baby into the storm drain, but I was just kidding! Don't be a tattletale.**❞**

tea (noun | /ti/):

The hot goss that your friend's been holding onto, like a literal cup of burning tea she's waiting to toss in your face when the time is right.

Origin: If there's anything that has withstood the test of time, it's Keanu Reeves. Oh, and also gossip. Men and women have been swapping stories of private affairs and bitter divorces since the Big Bang, whether it's over a few glasses of wine at dinner or around the watercooler with your other nosy coworkers. Southern women have been known to discuss the town's local news over a few glasses of afternoon tea, and, in fact, that's where this term came from.

> **❝**Girl, I saw you over there chatting up Jacob about his fangs. Spill the tea. Is he a werewolf or what? And is he seeing that vampire girl?**❞**

tennies (noun | /ˈtɛnɪz/):

Tennis shoes. The whiter-than-a-Jodi-Picoult-book-signing kind.

Origin: *Tennies* originated around 1951, which makes sense, because the only person still wearing them is your grandfather.

> 66 Ethel, dear, have you seen my tennies anywhere? Marty wants to play doubles today, and I can't find the stinkin' things anywhere! 99

thicc (adjective | /θɪk/):

Thicc people have so many curves, they needed an extra *c* added to the word. Get it? Because, curves. With a *c*. Forget it . . .

Origin: In 2015, the rise of the body positivity movement led to a surge in anatomy-related slang, like this salacious quip. Meme culture eventually got hold of *thicc*, displaying it across pictures of shapely cartoon characters and the like.

> 66 Have you ever noticed how thicc Mr. Krabs is? Look at those legs. Look at those eyeballs. 99

thirsty (adjective | /ˈθərsti/):

Desiring affection or attention, like your cat who sits on your face at 6:00 a.m. or your girlfriend who texts you thirty times in one afternoon "just to check in."

Origin: While we were all busy watching him "Superman," Soulja Boy was slipping this nugget into one of his other 2007 songs before promptly disappearing, like a ghost fulfilling its final wish.

thong (noun | /θɔŋ/):

A G-string for your feet, also known as flip-flops.

Origin: It appears that *thong* was a term for sandals up until the 1970s, at which point *flip-flops* took over and *thong* switched over to the fashion department, referring to underwear with a single strand that nestles into the butt cheeks, like floss in teeth. Rumor has it that this transition began when these scandalous undergarments were introduced in the late '70s, causing sandal companies to remarket their summertime shoes as flip-flops to avoid confusion between the two.

> **❝** I asked for thongs for Christmas, and all I got were these stupid flip-flops. **❞**

thread (noun | /θrɛd/):

A slang word for *outfit* that takes the idea of clothes far too literally, like if you were to call a tattoo a "skin stain" or glasses . . . well, "glasses," actually.

Origin: A 2000s word likely inspired by the cloth clothes are made from.

❝ Got myself a new set of threads yesterday. Look! A neon jumpsuit with a fox tail on the back. You like? ❞

townie (noun | /ˈtaʊni/):

Someone who stays behind in the town they were raised in, forgoing college or travel for the chance to angrily throw rocks at encroaching college students and visit the same tiny doughnut shop every single day until they die. These mythical creatures usually choose a visible place to congregate, like a public park or a Starbucks, to complain about local problems, like how Tony's Liquor closed ten minutes early or how the recent cover band at the weekly outdoor summer picnic was "just OK."

Welcome!
"THERE'S NOTHING TO DO" BUT SOME OF YOU STILL DON'T LEAVE!

Origin: Primarily used to distinguish outsiders (university students, tourists, carnies), *townie* appeared in the 1800s as a way for college kids to describe the cantankerous old folks who wouldn't stop terrorizing them for invading their space. The term traveled all around the globe before settling in Boston where (some say) it became a common name for residents of Charlestown, a rougher, heavily Irish neighborhood whose members can sometimes be found clashing with non-townies at a bar like O'Malley's or Patty's Parlour.

trash (verb | /træʃ/):

To completely destroy, either through physical actions or words. It's what one bad haircut will do to your confidence.

Origin: *Trash* as in "to ruin" appears to have started in the 1970s, though it's hard to identify why. Was it coined by bitter Gen Xers, who, upon entering their rebellious phase, realized just how fun it is to trash hotel rooms? Or maybe it was popularized by boxer Muhammad Ali, a famous trash-talker who went so far as to release a full-length diss-track-filled album around this time? Perhaps an angry Beagle owner shouted it in frustration after their dog trashed the kitchen by littering it with literal trash? The jury is still out.

> ❝I left the back door open by accident, and that pesky raccoon that I shooed away last week snuck in and trashed my living room. Bitter little brat.❞

trill (adjective | /trɪl/):

In the music world: a tremulous vibration. In the spherical object world: to spin around. In the slang word: a hybrid of true and real. (See: *realness*.)

Origin: Another contribution from the hip-hop world, *trill* was first dropped by the group UGK on their 1992 album *The Southern Way* as a complimentary title for someone who was considered authentic, sincere, and humble—someone who would "remember the little people" once they made it to the top.

> ❝In his Grammy acceptance speech, Gunther thanked his ninth-grade music teacher for inspiring him to pursue a career in bongo playing. What a trill guy.❞

trippin' (verb | /ˈtrɪpɪn/):

To be freaking out or panicking; what your brain starts doing when, thirty minutes into your sixty-minute drive, you remember that you left the stove on. Or did you? Surely, your roommate would have called, unless they left for Coachella already and forgot to tell you. Oh God, what if the building's burning down? Did you remember to pay the apartment insurance bill this month? Is your cat OK? Do you have a cat? You know what, probably best to call off work for the day and turn around—you can't risk it.

Origin: Unsurprisingly, *trippin'* was originally slang for "being extremely high"—a term that arose after the boom of hallucinatory drugs like LSD in the 1980s. This naturally led to the "erratic" definition, as those doped up on such substances tended to act buzzy or paranoid while they were under the influence. Over time, it began to be applied to those who had generally crazy ideas, like whoever thought it was a good idea to reboot *American Idol* not even ten years after the original ended. Really?

"Sorry, you want to 'just be friends' but you also want to keep using my Netflix account? Are you trippin'?"

troll (verb / noun | /troʊl/):

Someone who provokes others through inflammatory comments on the internet along the lines of "why does yerr face luk so dUMB?!"

Origin: In Norse mythology, trolls were big, bumbling creatures who hid in dark crannies waiting for an opportune time to jump out and inconvenience someone with riddles. Trolls these days do something similar, if you replace "dark crannies" with "the internet" and "inconvenience someone" with "make vicious attacks" and "bumbling creatures" with "angry men" and . . . well, you get the point.

truckin' (verb | /'trʌkɪn/):

To strut around with your head held high, a grin plastered across your face, and a stomping gait that suggests you're having the best gosh darn day of your human life.

Origin: This 1960s baby was ripped from a comic strip by an underground artist named R. Crumb, whose single-panel cartoons often featured cheerful men trotting around with big smiles, loose limbs, and carefree confidence. It reflects the optimistic, bold spirit of the counterculture movement and the joyful hippies that fueled it.

tubular (adjective| /ˈtjuːbjʊlə/):

Breathtaking, like the wave the dad who said it is probably cruising on.

Origin: By 1982, *tubular* had surfaced as a synonym for "good," inspired by the "tubes" that curling waves seemed to create during surfing season.

> ❝Dude, look at this straw. It's totally tubular, don't you think?❞

turnt (adjective | /təːrnt/):

When a vampire "turns" a human, they transform them into a bloodthirsty, coffin-dwelling monster. Similarly, when alcohol "turns" a human, it is transforming them into a loud-talking, spit-flinging, dance-loving monster. Maybe this comparison helps explain the thinking behind *turnt*: a party word for "intoxicated."

Origin: According to some lexicographers, the phrase (which appeared on Urban Dictionary in 2005) came from the phrase "to turn it up," another way of saying "let's get this party started." In 2008, Twitter came along and welcomed the word into its feed, eventually passing it along to the hip-hop world, which passed it along to the youths, which led to a slew of headlines like "How To Tell If You're Living Turnt" and "Oprah and Gayle King Unsure If Turnt Is Still A Slang."

❝I have three bottles of wine and the *Lost* DVDs if you want to get turnt with me tonight.❞

twerk (verb / noun | /twərk/):

A dance involving the rapid up-and-down movement of the buttocks that should never be attempted by anyone older than sixty or whiter than the foam on a caramel latte.

Origin: Likely a blend of the words *twist* and *jerk*, *twerk* has technically been around since the 1820s, first appearing in the form *twirk*. Over one hundred years later, the introduction of bounce music into the 1990s New Orleans music scene brought with it this gem, meant to describe the thrusting, shaking motions made by those who bravely tried to dance to this new genre. By 2013, *twerk* had officially been inducted into the dictionary, delighting music fans and Miley Cyrus alike.

"I WAS TWERKING AND I CAN'T GET UP!"

66 Mom, please stop twerking. You're wearing yoga pants and I can see every jiggle of your butt when you do it. 99

twihard (noun | /ˈtwaɪˌhɑrd/):

A *Twilight* enthusiast, one who tries hard to be normal but just can't resist the allure of sparkling men and baby-loving werewolves.

Origin: It feels pretty obvious, but just in case: *twihard* is a play on "try-hard" and *Twilight*, the best-selling vampire romance novel published in 2005 that caused a generation of kids to dream of marrying undead men.

SPECIAL DIRECTOR'S CUT!

BRUCE WILLIS IS NOT IN THIS

twiHARD

> ❝ Jessica, why are you covered in glitter and fake blood? Did you hurt yourself in art class today? Or are you becoming a twihard? Either way, go take a shower, please. ❞

twofer (noun | /ˈtuːfə/):

It's when you receive two items when you only expected one. Twofers can be good (a barista gives you two coffees for the price of one) or bad (a thug punches you in the face twice) or somewhere in between (you buy your girlfriend a ticket to a Jonas Brothers concert, and she surprises you with another one so you can join her).

Origin: Around the 1950s, it became common for theaters to offer a coupon entitling the holder to purchase two show tickets for the price of one in order to generate a larger crowd, leading to this humorous word (though the phrase that inspired it, *two for (one)*, dates back to 1900).

> ❝ They were offering twofer tattoos this weekend, so I got one on each cheek. And yes, it's the cheek you're thinking of. ❞

upchuck (verb | /ˈʌptʃʌk/):

To vomit up all thirty-six bags of Skittles that you drunkenly ate last night. See the rainbow, taste the rainbow.

Origin: While the jokester in me wants to believe that it came from a mid-hello snafu ("What's up, Chuck-BLARFFFFFWDKRQNCOR?"), the academic in me knows better. In reality, *upchuck* (a 1936 American word) comes from the simple blend of *up* and *chuck*, as if one is chucking (throwing) one's insides up into the air, showering neighboring friends and strangers with last night's dinner, to their dismay.

> ❝ I upchucked over her new white couch, fell asleep in it, and woke up stuck to the fabric like a fly on sticky paper. It was not my favorite Halloween. ❞

V (adjective | /vi/):

The twenty-second letter of the modern English alphabet, the twentieth letter of the Roman alphabet, and the abbreviated form of the word *very* that your seventeen-year-old will slip into a text at some point in the near future.

Origin: This linguistic blip can mostly be traced to textese—the clipped language born from the strict 140-character limit that many early cell phones imposed on their users. When Twitter came out, bringing with it a similar 140-character restriction, *v* switched platforms, dragging acronyms like *OMG* and *LOL* over to this new, blue digital landscape. But if we're talking about when *v* first appeared (not when it became popular), then we have to go all the way back to the 1800s, when it was cited in an issue of *The Horticultural Review and Botanical Magazine* to describe crop conditions (v good, v bad, v croppy).

> ❝ I'm v excited about going to the b this weekend. P sure it's going to be sun-e, so bring the ss or else you'll turn r. ❞

vamoose (verb | /væˈmus/):

A common Dad-ism for "Let's get movin', kids. Put your video games away and get your sneakers on. Your mom and I are going to teach you about the great outdoors!"

Origin: This verb for "to leave hurriedly" is an adaptation of the third-person Spanish conjugation *vamos* meaning "let's go." Though some believe that it came across the border from Mexico, others cite the word in American newspapers and even British newspapers much earlier, going as far back as 1827, when author William Clarke urged his friends to "vamos" and move away from a bunch of strange creatures at a local fair.

vape (verb / noun | /veɪp/):

To smoke an electronic cigarette, inviting the judgment and scorn of the hipster coffee shop patrons around you, who would prefer that you puff on your little battery outside, please. Yes, they know that the smoke is water vapor and no, they don't care.

Origin: Smoking has been an American pastime for centuries, blackening the lungs of its users long before they knew better. But it wasn't until 1927 that someone (in this case, a man named Joseph Robinson) proposed an electronic approach to slowly killing yourself; in May of that year, he filed a patent (with pictures!) pitching an idea for what he called an electric vaporizer that would burn "medicinal compounds" for "health benefits." Since then, many ciggy scientists have tried and failed to invent an e-cigarette that consumers weren't embarrassed to be seen with. It wasn't until 2003 when a man named Hon Lik debuted his pen-sized e-cig that the practice finally took off, exploding across international markets and finding its way into the hands of teenagers, who promptly dubbed the term *vaping*.

> 66 Don't blow that vape smoke in my face, bro. I don't care if it's organic. 99

vlog (verb / noun | /vlag/):

A blog (digital diary) composed of video footage of one's daily life. No matter what you vlog about—makeup collections, movie reviews, a literal cardboard box—you will most likely find an audience because the internet is vast and strange, just like you.

Origin: Widely credited to Adam Kontras, who, upon graduating in 2000, embarked on a road trip to Los Angeles in hopes of joining "the biz." Every day, the man composed a blog entry describing his journey and paired it with a brief video clip. Though Kontras's dreams of making it big eventually fizzled, the practice he invented— *vlogging*, or "video blogging"—didn't and has, ironically, become a legitimate entertainment career.

vom (verb / noun | /vam/):

To, in the simplest sense, vomit.

Origin: Supposedly, an '80s word and one of the dozens of nicknames for vomit, many of which are in this book. (Sorry.)

> **"I vommed all over the cat yesterday.
> She hasn't looked at me since."**

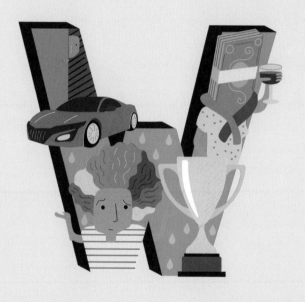

W (noun | /ˈdʌb(ə)ljuː/):

A win, either a literal one (you beat your opponent in a soccer tournament) or a metaphorical one (you spoke to your crush for five minutes straight before blurting out something bizarre).

Origin: Similar to *v* and *P*, *W* sprouted from the early days of texting, where you had to choose your characters carefully to avoid sending truncated messages like "There's something I have to tell you. I'm- (1/58)."

> **❝** Gotta get that W, boys, or else Coach is going to be V mad at us. **❞**

waspy (adjective | /ˈwɑspi/):

Old money, old-fashioned, and frankly, old, at least at heart. Waspy people often cherish their cultured tastes, proper manners, and first-world problems. They wear salmon pink polos from Ralph Lauren, own boats they only take pictures with, and become both confused and peeved when you point out either. They own a beach house, and it's probably in the Hamptons.

Origin: Originally an acronym for White Anglo-Saxon Protestant, *WASP* or *waspy* describes a person who is, well, white, of European descent, and religious. Unfortunately, it has a long history of negative connotations; in one of its earliest mentions, Charles Lewis Fowler uses it to describe the Ku Klux Klan and the growth of racist, anti-Semitic groups in the South who were often very All of the Above. This is not necessarily to say that current WASPs are racist, anti-Semitic, rich, and white, but simply to say that's where they started. What happened afterward, I cannot speak to.

wassup (int. | /(h)wəˈsəp/):

A greeting that should always be pronounced with a prolonged ending to signify just how chill you are.

Origin: On December 20, 1999, Budweiser beer aired a commercial that featured a bunch of friends parroting the slurred phrase *wassup* (a.k.a. "what's up"). The ad became a worldwide phenomenon, inspiring countless parodies and landing the slang word in the proverbial pop-culture hall of fame.

❝ Wassssssupppppp. ❞

whack (adjective | /hwak/):

Crazy, like the person who inexplicably whacked you in the face with a fly swatter and walked away.

Origin: First appearing in the early eighteenth century as a verb for "to hit," *whack* joined the league of "criminal underworld slang" as a word for "one's share of the goods or money." This idea of one's "fair share" evolved to eventually mean "a fair agreement" and then, later, "in fair shape." Over time, the definition naturally flipped (like how *literally* came to mean "figuratively") and morphed into a term for "in poor shape," which is why we call things that malfunction (computers, toasters, people) "out of whack." By the late 1900s, *whack* had taken on a new noun form for something that's absurd.

whip (noun | /hwɪp/):

A cool car, the kind you want to whip your hair back and forth in.

Origin: Back in the days of stagecoaches, travelers who were in a hurry could, with the flick of the wrist, up their speed by administering a light whip to the steed. When cars were introduced, "the whip" became synonymous with the steering wheel and, eventually, with the car itself.

> **"** Five-cent pizza down on Fairfax? Well, what are we waiting for? Let's whip this whip around and get some grub, boys! **"**

wicked (adverb | /ˈwɪkɪd/):

Exceedingly or very; a New England baby's first word.

Origin: Bostonians will claim this word as their own and, frankly, they have good reason to. During the Salem Witch Trials of the 1600s, Puritans in Massachusetts launched a crusade against women that they believed to be cursed or "wicked," thus cementing the term's place in the state's lexicon. Over time, this adjective for *awful* evolved into an adverb for *awfully*, which quickly lodged itself into the vocabularies of every chest-pounding Masshole.

wig (verb | /wɪg/):

To freak out or display signs of stress indicative of an impending breakdown. You know someone is wigging out if their face is flushed, their body is shaking, and they're repeatedly whispering dramatic phrases to themselves like "oh no, oh no, oh no" or "Mom's never going to forgive me for this."

Origin: The word *wig* comes from the word *periwig*, which refers to the "clump of artificial hair that one sticks atop their head, either to hide early onset baldness or to look sophisticated." (See: *bigwig*.) By the turn of the twentieth century, wig had come to describe, not only the hair on one's head but one's actual, literal head, which is how the term "wigging out" developed—if someone was "flipping their wig," it meant they were losing their mind. If someone was "on their way to wig city" it meant they were acting crazy. Eventually, all of these negative connotations snowballed into one big catchall phrase: "wigging out." And there you have it.

> **"** The date was going well until I realized that she didn't like *Star Wars* and I kinda, sorta wigged out on her. **"**

willy-nilly (adverb | /ˈwɪlɪˈnɪli/):

Haphazardly or without regard for your mother's very careful instructions that she relayed to you at least three times in the hopes that maybe, just maybe, you would listen this time.

Origin: In a perfect world, *willy-nilly* would have a quaint little origin, like "it was named after a very silly boy named Willy," but that's not the reality we're living in. No, this adjective instead comes from a contraction of "will I, nill I," the 1608 way of saying "will he or won't he," hence the word's ties to indecision or recklessness.

  ❝ Sweetheart, you can't keep spending money all willy-nilly. We have bills to pay and kids to feed and, like, five streaming subscriptions to maintain. ❞

win (verb / noun | /wɪn/):

To succeed at a particular task, whether big ("I'm winning at life") or small ("I'm winning at breathing"). Can also be a noun for "a positive result," as in "I had a big win today, boys—I ate an entire salad, croutons and all").

Origin: It's hard to nail down when *win* went slang, considering the term's been around longer than most of our vocabulary (per the *Oxford English Dictionary*, it first appeared around 1175). One theory suggests that it evolved out of the phrase "for the win," popularized by the 1966 game show *Hollywood Squares* in which contestants gunnin' for the big prize had to utter the phrase "for the win" in order to make a move. Another theory claims the word originated in rugby, when players, faced with the choice of running the ball for two points versus kicking it for one, were encouraged "to go for the win" regardless of the risks. Yet another theory places the word in online, multiplayer games like *World of Warcraft* around the early 2000s. So, we'll leave this one up to you.

wiseacre (noun | /ˈwaɪzˌeɪkər/):

A smart alec. Not like a smart guy named Alec, though I'm sure those do exist. I'm certainly not denying the existence of Smart Alecs. Don't twist my words. You know what, just get out, OK? I don't like your tone.

Origin: Not to be confused with *wisecracker* (another quip for a show-off), *wiseacre* comes from the Middle Dutch *wijssegger* ("soothsayer"), which accidentally became associated with the Middle Dutch *segger* ("sayer"). That then became mixed up with the obsolete English word *segger* (also "sayer"), which sometimes meant "braggart," which led to this nickname for know-it-alls.

❝Oh, you think you know everything, huh? You little wiseacre? OK, what number am I thinking of? Thirty-seven? *Wrong!*❞

woke (adjective | /woʊk/):

Up-to-date on cultural or social trends. Someone who is *woke* has an awareness of the world around them and the various ways in which it is slowly crumbling. That thirteen-year-old climate change activist? Woke. The head of the local university's community volunteer group? Woke. Your dog who loves everyone equally regardless of their questionable fashion choices? *Definitely* woke.

Origin: American singer-songwriter Erykah Badu released a song in 2008 called "Master Teacher" in which she preaches self-awareness by using the phrase "I stay woke." This idea of always staying on your toes and being in the know was eventually adopted by the Black Lives Matter movement in the 2010s, a time when discrimination against African Americans was seemingly on the rise and widely publicized. Black Lives Matter advocates who were particularly vocal were considered *woke*, leading to the term's association with activism and "fighting the good fight."

wuss (noun | /wʊs/):

Courage the Cowardly Dog. Millhouse. Neville Longbottom. You, nervously sweating at the bar the second a cowboy strides in. All of these people are *wusses*: timid, scared, or in some cases, downright weak people. Come on, now, no need to cry about it . . .

Origin: A bully's favorite zinger, *wuss* was plucked directly from the cult classic *Fast Times at Ridgemont High*, in which the sly Mike Damone mockingly calls someone a "wuss: part wimp and part pussy." (Pussy being another derogatory name for a scaredy-cat.)

> **"**Are you going to be a wuss, or are you going to touch the bee's nest? I don't have all day.**"**

XOXO (noun | /ɛksoʊɛksoʊ/):

Kisses and hugs; what you write to your crush at the end of your Valentine to hint at your admiration while also playing it cool.

XYZ (int. | /ɛkshwʌɪzi/):

An abbreviation used to signal to someone that they should zip up their pants or else risk exposing their underpants to the general population.

Origin: Albeit more of a phrase than a single word, *XYZ* is an abbreviation for "examine your zipper" ("eXamine Your Zipper"). This witticism appeared during the 1960s, but its etymology beyond that is unclear.

> **" Mr. President, before you start your State of the Union speech, you should probably . . . ahem . . . XYZ."**

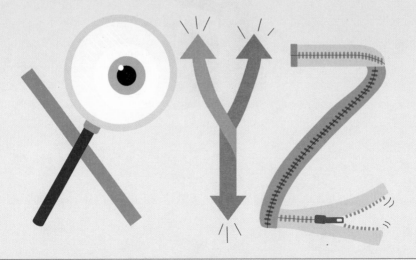

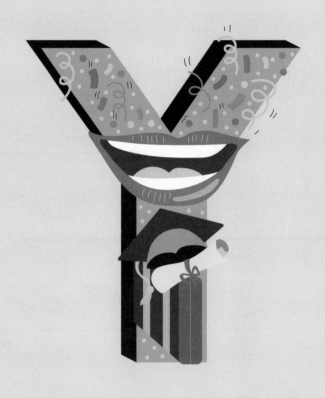

yap (verb | /jæp/):

To talk loudly or incessantly, like a dog who has just laid eyes on the mailman.

Origin: Speaking of dogs, their earsplitting yelps were the original inspiration for this word. It first appeared in the 1600s to describe pups whose barks sounded like "yaps."

yas (adverb | /jæs/):

The word yes, but cooler.

Origin: Another word borrowed from 1980s ball culture (see: *kween*), yas was first introduced by drag queens as a way to encourage fellow performers on stage, similar to "You go, girl!" It lingered around the LGBTQ and African American communities until the 2010s, when it went mainstream thanks to both an enthusiastic Lady Gaga fan, who shouted the term at the pop star in a now viral video as she was leaving an event one night, and Ilana Glazer, who made the term a staple of her Broad City character's vocabulary.

> **❝** Yasssssssss, we stan you, kween!
> Slay that stage, my baller BBG! **❞**

yeet (int. | /jit/):

An expression of excitement, glee, or in some cases, simple acknowledgment.

Origin: Go back to 2014, when Russia was butchering the Olympics and every kid under the age of seventeen was on a social media app called Vine. One such kid, a tween named Lil' Meatball, posted a video of himself doing a dance he dubbed the Yeet. Soon, it was seized by the internet as a positive exclamation similar to *yas* or *amen*. Frequently used when completing a successful dance move or basketball shot, or while throwing something, *yeet* has wiggled its way into every corner of the World Wide Web, confusing parents and millennials alike.

> **"** See this phone? See that ocean? YEET! Now it's sleepin' with the fishes. **"**

yuppie

(noun | /ˈjəpi/):

A working, young, urban professional who can be seen wearing button-ups, backpacks, and AirPods at all hours of the day; cherishes their Macbook Air; and can't go five seconds without chattering about the latest music festival they went to. Hated by blue-collar workers and championed by liberal elites, these walking college pamphlets are divisive figures due to their affluence and perceived sense of entitlement.

Origin: Coined in the 1980s by writer John Epstein of *The American Scholar*. Or was it journalist Dan Rottenberg in Chicago magazine? Honestly, we're unsure, as are most people, but one thing that is certain is how despised the OG yuppies of the Gen X era were. These young professionals were known for landing high-paying jobs in the city, buying brownstones, and flaunting their flashy startup job salaries in the form of designer slacks and gaudy cars. The term has made a resurgence in recent years thanks to the Silicon Valley boom, which has sent hoards of fresh-faced computer geeks into cities like San Francisco, where they start earning upward of two-hundred-thousand dollars fresh out of college and shack up in million-dollar condos that most of us can only dream about.

66 This city is being taken over by yuppies. Just the other day, I saw five new Starbucks pop up filled with charging stations and probiotic juices with names like Cleanse and Unity to satisfy these rich little monsters. 99

zaddy (noun | /ˈzædi/):

An attractive older man that you wouldn't mind discussing the economic crisis with over a glass of aged bourbon before nuzzling into his chest hair and falling asleep to the latest NPR episode humming quietly in the background of his Pottery Barn–furnished bedroom.

Origin: *Zaddy* is the new *Silver Fox.* Which is to say, it describes an attractive older man with swag who dresses well, eats right, and never leaves the house without kissing you goodbye. First mentioned in the Ty Dolla $ign's 2016 song of the same name, *zaddy* is a title held by many Hollywood hotties, including Jon Hamm, Jon Hamm, and definitely Jon Hamm.

> **❝** I just want a zaddy that owns a fitted tux
> and will help me file my taxes. **❞**

zeek (noun | /zik/):

A geek with sex appeal, like if you put Sheldon Cooper in Chris Pine's body.

Origin: Described by one Urban Dictionary user as "geek to the power of seven," *zeek* supposedly appeared in the 1980s to describe an attractive dork, though no one can seem to track down its origin, making it as questionable as the existence of zeeks themselves.

> **"**Why settle for regular geeks when you could hold out for the holy grail: a zeek?**"**

zinger (noun | /ˈzɪŋər/):

Something outstandingly good, especially a witty joke or caustic clapback that elicits a quiet "oh snap" from bystanders.

Origin: Once a baseball term for "fastball," *zinger* took on a punch-line definition in the 1970s, combining the term *zing* and the suffix *-er*.

> **"**Eminem kept hitting me with zingers until I was eventually booed off the stage. Yet another lost rap battle.**"**

zippo (noun | /ˈzɪpəʊ/):

How much spending money your dad plans on giving you for your trip to the mall later. Which is to say, zero. Nothing. Nought. Zilch. Nada. Zip. Get a job.

Origin: In 1900, students seeking a tamer way to describe their failing test scores settled on *zip* and later, *zippo* (which is really just *zip* with pizzazz).

zoned (adjective | /zəʊnd/):

Also known as *zoned out*, used to describe anyone who appears mentally absent due to drugs, alcohol, or sleep deprivation caused by a foolish attempt to watch all eight Harry Potter movies back-to-back.

Origin: Like most words related to intoxication, *zoned* was coined during the drug haze that was the 1960s. It was modeled after *ozone* with the suggestion being that if one was *zoned out*, they had their head in the clouds.

> **“**I zoned out for my entire Anthropology class yesterday, a full sixty-one minutes. That's gotta be a new record.**”**

zombie (noun | /ˈzɑmbi/):

A creature that loves humans and feeds on their flesh, or a human that hates creatures and feeds on boredom.

Origin: While this slang for "a dull, personality-less person" has been circulating since the 1940s, its roots run much deeper, back to the 1800s when members of West Indies tribes believed that zombies were people who came back from the dead, but without their souls.

zonked (adjective | /zɒŋkt/):

Exhausted or worn-out. Not to be confused with *zoinks*, the catch-phrase of everyone's favorite cartoon beatnik, Shaggy Rogers.

Origin: Yet another Americanism from the 1960s, *zonked* started out as a word for intoxicated, as many under the influence of drugs or alcohol would *zonk out* (pass out). Eventually, it shifted from describing intoxication to this tired, "passing out" post-intoxication phrase.

> **❝**I'd love to come to your friend's game night, Mandy, but my neighbor's been practicing his banjo every night this week until 3:00 a.m., so I'm feeling positively zonked.**❞**

zoot (noun | /zut/):

A large, exaggerated suit made out of loose, often bright clothing. You might've seen it in the WWII chapter of your history textbook or in Jim Carrey's 1994 film *The Mask*.

Origin: During the 1940s, America was instructed to ration food and goods in order to support the war effort, including textiles like clothing. In retaliation against the violence, some men decided to stand up to Uncle Sam by donning extravagant outfits (zoot suits) that used far more fabric than the government approved of. As a result, these groups (and the zoots that they wore) earned them some negative labels like "anti-American" and "rebellious."

zozzled (adjective | /ˈzɑz(ə)ld/):

One of the many words for intoxicated that confirms my theory that America really needs to lay off the margaritas for a while.

Origin: In 1886, *sozzled* (from the word *sozzle* for "to splash") was used to describe those who, after one too many alcoholic beverages, promptly became sloppy and prone to spilling their drink all over the place. The word reappeared in a new form, *zozzled*, during the Prohibition era in the 1920s, which is not all that surprising.

    ❝I wish I could say 'it was the best night of my life,' but I was zozzled for most of it and can't remember a thing.❞

Acknowledgments

As we publish the third book in the *Illustrated Compendium* series, I must once again thank my publisher John Whalen for placing his trust on some Bostonian he found on the internet and my editor Margaret McGuire Novak for keeping that Bostonian in check. I also want to thank the illustrious Rebecca Pry, whose endless well of creativity and humor has made even my worst jokes look hilarious.

Also, to my friends who have now put up with three books' worth of questions about ugly adjectives, strange nouns, and obnoxious slang: thank you for all of your suggestions and for practically ghostwriting these gift books with me.

Most of all, thank you to my family, who grew tired of my jokes years ago but continue to support me. I wish I could say I won't write any embarrassing stories about you in the future, but that would be a lie.

And lastly, I'd like to thank the Starbucks at the Sherman Oaks Galleria, which has robbed me of hundreds of dollars in cold brew during the last few strenuous months of this project. I want to say if I had the chance to do it all over again, I wouldn't spend half of my paycheck on your iced coffees, but we both know that's not true, so thanks for keeping me alive, I guess.

About the Author

Tyler Vendetti is a writer and media guru whose work focuses on pop culture, humor, and the trials and tribulations of twentysomething-hood. Author of and *The Illustrated Compendium of Weirdly Specific Words* and *The Illustrated Compendium of Ugly English Words*—this book's predecessors—Tyler is a contributor to xoJane, TIME Online, *Cosmopolitan* magazine, HelloGiggles, The Penny Hoarder, and Thought Catalog, among others. She currently works in the entertainment business, assisting writers and producers at companies like NBCUniversal, Warner Bros., and Netflix. (This is a humblebrag and she knows it.) A comedy enthusiast with a flair for horror, Tyler can be found on Twitter @HeyThereFuture or at her poorly decorated Los Angeles apartment.

About the Illustrator

Rebecca Pry is an illustrator and designer living in Warwick, New York. She received a BFA in illustration from Rhode Island School of Design in 2013. Rebecca's art adds a humorous twist to everyday items and scenes, and she has created patterns and graphics for home goods, books, accessories, and apparel. She regularly shows her work in local galleries in the Hudson Valley. When she is not drawing, she is outside in a brightly colored sweater. See more at rebeccapry.com.

PUBLISHING PRACTICAL & CREATIVE NONFICTION

Whalen Book Works is a small, independent book publishing company
based in Kennebunkport, Maine, that combines top-notch design, unique formats,
and fresh content to create truly innovative gift books.

Our unconventional approach to bookmaking is a close-knit, creative, and
collaborative process among authors, artists, designers, editors, and booksellers.
We publish a small, carefully curated list each season, and we take the time
to make each book exactly what it needs to be.

We believe in giving back. That's why we plant one tree for every ten books
sold. Your purchase supports a tree in the Rocky Mountain National Park.

Get in touch!

Visit us at **Whalenbooks.com**
or write to us at
68 North Street, Kennebunkport, ME 04046

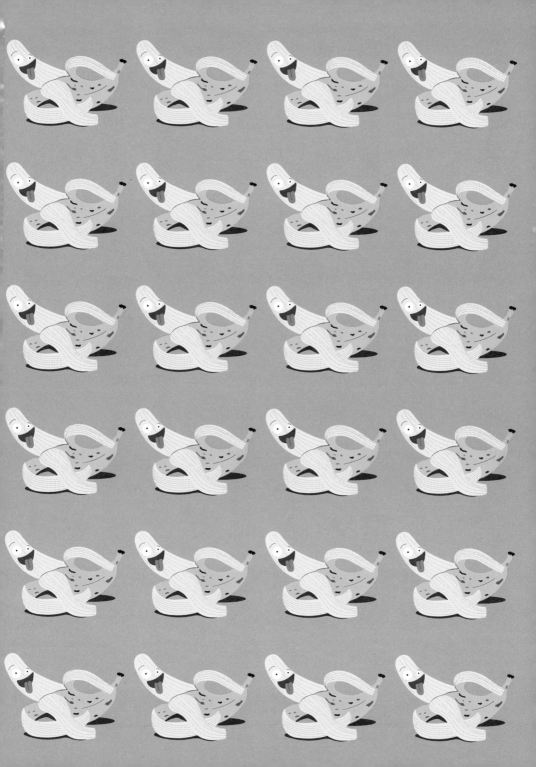